I0048722

ALSO BY LAURENS BENSDORP

AUTOMATED STOCK TRADING SYSTEMS:
*A Systematic Approach for Traders to Make Money in Bull,
Bear and Sideways Markets*

THE 30-MINUTE STOCK TRADER:
The Stress-Free Trading System for Financial Freedom

TRADING
RETIREMENT
ACCOUNTS

AUTOMATED SYSTEMS TO MAKE MONEY IN BULL
AND SIDEWAYS MARKETS, PRESERVE YOUR WEALTH
IN BEAR MARKETS, AND GUARD AGAINST INFLATION

LAURENS BENSDORP

PUBLISHED BY AVOCET BOOKS
www.avocetbooks.com

COPYRIGHT © 2025 LAURENS BENSDORP
All rights reserved. This book or parts thereof may not be reproduced in any form, stored in any retrieval system, or transmitted in any form by any means—electronic, mechanical, photocopy, recording, or otherwise—without prior written permission of the author, except as provided by United States of America copyright law.

ISBN:

Hardcover	978-1-963678-16-1
Paperback	978-1-963678-14-7
eBook	978-1-963678-15-4

First Edition

BOOK PRODUCTION BY AVOCET BOOKS
www.avocetbooks.com

By reading this document, the reader agrees that under no circumstances is the author or the publisher responsible for any losses, direct or indirect, which are incurred as a result of the use of information contained within this document, including, but not limited to, errors, omissions, or inaccuracies.

LEGAL NOTICE:
This book is copyright protected. Please note the information contained within this document is for educational and personal use only. You cannot amend, distribute, sell, use, quote or paraphrase any part, or the content within this book, without the consent of the author.

Disclaimer

The methods, techniques and systems shared in this book are not guaranteed to be profitable and may result in losses. Past results are not necessarily indicative of future results. Examples presented in this book are for educational purposes only. The representations in this book are not solicitations of any order to buy or sell. The author, the publisher, and all affiliates assume no responsibility for your trading results. There is a high degree of risk in trading.

Hypothetical or simulated performance results have certain inherent limitations. Unlike an actual performance record, simulated results do not represent actual trading. Also, since the trades have not been executed, the results may have under- or overcompensated for the impact, if any, of certain market factors, such as lack of liquidity. Simulated trading programs in general are designed with the benefit of hindsight and do not represent the future. No representation is made in this book that any trading system will or is likely to achieve profits or losses similar to those shown.

TABLE OF CONTENTS

CHAPTER 1

THE RETIREMENT ACCOUNT DILEMMA

"I WAS COMPLETELY UNPREPARED FOR WHAT HAPPENED IN THE stock market 2022," an investor wrote to me.

"It was a particularly difficult year for me as I was extremely busy building a second home out of state, which led to me completely taking my eye off the ball with my portfolio and the market.

"My personal portfolio was down over 35 percent in 2022, which was my biggest decline in any calendar year. Because I did not want to take my eye off the ball again the way I had in 2022, I felt like I had to be at my desk every minute of the day so I would 'not miss anything.' This led to difficult times at home as I didn't feel like I had time for anything else but keeping a close eye on my life savings and the stock market. My relationship with my wife suffered."

Does that story sound familiar? The year 2022 was especially hard for buy-and-hold investors. It was made harder by the fact that the traditional 60-40 equities-bonds approach that so many investors had learned stopped working when both the stock and bond markets declined.

Maybe you did all right in 2022—good for you if you did. But what about March 2020? Or 2018? Or 2011? Or 2008? Because here's the thing: *Markets go down*. The traditional advice for individual investors in these situations is to hold on, don't worry, the market will come back. Well, after 2008, when the market declined more than 50 percent, it needed almost *five years* to come back—to simply recoup your losses to where your accounts were before that crash. Investors who are retired or nearing retirement don't have that kind of runway. These investors are dissatisfied with the results they achieve through traditional buy-and-hold investing. They understand that nineteen out of twenty investment managers underperform the market, and they don't like the pain of riding out the inevitable downturns that come with investing in low-cost index funds. Plus they have to worry about inflation, which is back after more than a generation of being almost nonexistent.

On the other hand, they don't want to be chained to their computers, gut-grinding every day about whether they are about to lose their nest egg, like the investor who wrote me the letter above. Simply put, they want better investment performance and more peace of mind.

If that sounds like you, even a little bit, keep reading.

Constraints of Trading Retirement Accounts

Many individual investors hold Individual Retirement Accounts (IRAs), Roth IRAs, or self-directed 401(k) accounts (for purposes of this book I group all of these under the term *retirement accounts*). Their retirement nest egg may represent their largest account of all, but they cannot fully implement the systems I teach in my first two books on systematic trading because of regulations unique to retirement accounts.

Specifically, they are not allowed to trade short—that is, to bet that a stock will fall. Moreover, all the strategies I have taught in previous books involve trading on margin so that investors can trade short and long simultaneously. They can't do that in retirement accounts either.

I wrote this, my third book on systematic trading strategies, for investors who face these constraints. They do not want to rely on fundamental analytics, predictions, or stock picking because they understand, either through educating themselves or bitter experience, that those approaches don't work consistently over time when it comes to beating the market. They want something that is better performing, more consistent, and more reliable. While I have focused the teachings in this book on US readers who manage individual retirement accounts, the principles and approach I teach in the following pages are valid for any investor managing any kind of trading account.

The core principle to my approach is this: ***Combinations of noncorrelated stock trading systems can make more money, more consistently, than market indices.*** They comprise different types of trading styles such that when some are losing money, others are making money. In combination, they aim to produce a smoother, more consistent equity curve that is less volatile than the market and shows higher returns and lower drawdowns.

I'll show you more about this concept and how it works in the next chapter.

Retirement Investors Are in a Bind

Three binds, really.

Imagine you had a $2 million retirement account in 2007. You might look at that and think, "Okay, over the long term the market generally returns about 8 percent a year, I can retire on this and live off the returns." A year later, if you had a buy-and-hold strategy and only held an S&P 500 index fund, your retirement account would be worth less than half what it had been (56 percent less, in fact). If this account was your principal source of income, you wouldn't be able to maintain your standard of living. The opportunity to retire would recede into the distant future. If you already had retired, you might need to go look for a job or start consulting. On top of that, you faced the task of *doubling* your remaining money just to get back to where you had been before, a daunting task in a good market, much less 2009. That kind of experience can be devasting; the prospect of it is terrifying. "Running out of money" is a top fear of retirees. This is why retirement account investors are so concerned about not losing their principal. The implications of a substantial loss of equity for those who are later in life are much more serious than for younger investors who have time to recoup losses.

Second, retirement account investors worry about inflation eating into their returns and purchasing power. If you want to have the same purchasing power in 2024 as you had in 2019, you need 23 percent more income. This is shocking to anyone who hasn't lived through inflation, and the last significant inflationary period in the United States was almost fifty years ago.

Third, they want to outperform the major indices, but they don't have a lot of runway to do so. In the first quarter of 2020, for example, the S&P 500 dropped 33 percent. Retirement account investors simply can't afford to take a hit like that and climb out of the resulting hole. They have to find a way to dodge those drops and keep growing their assets.

Yet retirement account investors work with one hand tied behind their backs because of the trading limitations placed on their accounts. Without the ability to short stocks, they are particularly exposed to downturns—and downturns happen.

Bear Market Realities

Bear markets like what happened in 2022 are not out of the ordinary; they happen regularly. Here are some of the better-known ones:

- The crash of 1929–1932, in which the S&P 500 lost 85 percent of its value and took twenty-five years to recover.

- No performance between 1964 to 1982, when the net performance of the S&P 500 average was zero and inflation ate away 70 percent of purchasing power.

- The 1987 crash, in which stocks fell 21 percent in a single day.

- The bear market from 2000 to 2003, also called the dotcom crash, in which the S&P 500 fell 49 percent; that decline lasted eighty-four months before returning to its high.

- The 2008 collapse that cost the S&P 500 56 percent of its value.

- The COVID crash, when the market fell 33 percent in one month.

- The inflation-and-pandemic-driven bear market that lopped off 20 percent of the S&P's value in 2022.

The evidence is crystal clear that bear markets are part of normal market behavior. Yet psychologically, many traders don't want to think about or remember them. We much prefer to expect things to go well, and most of us have a strong cognitive bias in that direction. History shows that this is a dangerous gamble, and it's not one you have to take, even—or especially—as a retirement account investor.

In this book I'll show how to trade your retirement account to make money in bull and sideways markets and *protect your money* in bear markets. You may be on the sidelines for a while, but that's fine because you'll preserve your capital. These retirement account trading systems are designed to prevent you from having to dig out of a big hole because you suffered a significant loss. Instead of having to make 50 percent or 100 percent just to get back to where you were, you will tread water until the market turns around and then start making money again, putting you far ahead of the major indices and bringing you a lot more peace of mind.

It's also important for you as a retiree or near-retiree to maintain your purchasing power, particularly if you are managing your retirement account to generate steady income for your support. Forty-five years ago, we experienced inflation that's almost unimaginable today: 14.8 percent (measured according to the consumer price index, or CPI) in March 1980. After that, there was very little inflation until the pandemic. When inflation reared up in 2021, people were very, very unhappy. We have no way of knowing the future, but it's wise to assume that we will see inflationary times again and to be prepared.

The systematic trading approach I teach in this book for trading retirement accounts can do all of these things.

A Better Way

Without the ability to short stocks, retirement investors lack one of the most useful tools for managing their investments during bear markets. When the market goes down, stocks become very correlated, which limits our options for making money and protecting capital. As you'll see in the coming chapters, we can deal with that limitation by developing an approach that makes money in bull and sideways markets. For bear markets, we design additional systems in such a way that they get out of the market during a downturn to preserve your equity. In simplest terms, you will be in the market and making money during bull and sideways periods but go partially or entirely to cash and sit on the sidelines during bear markets. The net effect is that you will make money when you can, protect your capital when you have to, avoid going into significant drawdowns, and experience greater peace of mind than I expect you do now.

I will lead you through a quantified approach to building seven complementary, noncorrelated systems simultaneously. This approach is much more robust than a buy-and-hold strategy to investing for a variety of reasons. At the most basic level, you will build trading systems that buy and sell stocks under different sets of rules. These rules take advantage of different market conditions and stock conditions. When conditions are such that some of your systems are making money, others may be losing money or on the sidelines—and that's not only okay, it's intentional. Gains in some systems offset losses in others. By dividing your capital among these systems and building systems that complement each other, the weaknesses of one approach are offset by the strengths of another, and you end up with an aggregate positive return. You also end up with reduced drawdowns relative to the broader market. Put it all together and you will have a compound annual growth rate that does better than the market, lesser drawdowns for shorter periods of time than the market, and lower volatility than the market.

Perhaps most important of all, you will reclaim your time—the one thing you can't get back. Rather than feeling you must be glued to your computer screen, constantly managing your investments, you can enjoy your retirement. Once you set up your trading systems, it is possible to do everything you need to do each trading day in thirty minutes or less. Then you can shut your computer off and go about your day with confidence about your retirement investments.

These are quantitative trading systems, which means we take a fundamentally different approach to investing from most investors and most of the financial media. We don't care about the news. We don't care about the strength of the management team or the earnings report or the way a strong currency affects overseas markets except in one important way: we care about how the stock moves. That's called "price action," and it's all that we concern ourselves with. A stock will move. We don't care why, only that it moves. Stocks move in somewhat predictable ways, and there is data about that movement. Quantitative analysis limits itself to seeking patterns in that data and ignores any whiff of trying to judge what the stock will do based on outside factors like earnings reports or news events. By finding patterns in that movement, we find a trading edge. We can quantify the conditions under which we will buy and sell a stock that produce a greater than average chance of making a profit.

The best part of this approach is that we can remove human judgment and human emotion from the equation. We don't have to guess what the stock is going to do; we study what it has done in the past and make an educated investment based on the understanding that some version of that behavior can be foreseen. Computers do this work for us.

The simulation of systems I describe in this book generated a simulated compound average annual growth rate from 2003 to September 30, 2024, of over 20 percent with the largest drawdown being 15 percent, but this is only one example

of what you can achieve. What I share with you here is a map
of where you can go; you can and should find your own way
using what I teach in these pages rather than try to mimic
what I've done. (More about why I give this advice below.)
While I make no promises about the performance of your systems, it is reasonable to expect that you can build systems that
over time deliver roughly twice the compound annual growth
rate of the broader market indices while experiencing less
severe, shorter drawdowns.

How I Learned to Trade

I have been teaching individual investors systematic trading
strategies since 2013. I wrote two books for these investors:
*The 30-Minute Stock Trader: The Stress-Free Trading
Strategy for Financial Freedom* (2017) and *Automated Stock
Trading Systems: A Systematic Approach for Traders to
Make Money in Bull, Bear and Sideways Markets* (2020).
I was able to write those books only because I have spent
decades developing and refining a systematic trading approach.

In the year 2000 I took over the job of managing our
family portfolio after the investment bankers advising us did
a terrible job. I fired them and decided I would learn how to
invest money myself. This was just as the dotcom crash was
beginning. Conventional wisdom advised me to sit tight, to
stay in our investments, that the market would come back.
As I looked at what was happening to Enron and WorldCom—
big companies that had been the darlings of Wall Street and
were now on their way to being worth nothing—I decided I
didn't believe the conventional wisdom. I didn't want to

follow the herd. I went straight to 100 percent cash. If I didn't know how to make money in the market, I wasn't going to stay invested and lose it. While we did lose some money, we would have lost a lot more if I hadn't done that.

As I continued to educate myself, I learned that most investing is based on fundamentals analysis, which is a fancy term for making an educated guess about the future. I wasn't comfortable with that approach. I wanted evidence, which meant looking at the past, analyzing market history to see what had happened, and seeking out patterns. Relying on historical market data, I could backtest trading algorithms, applying a set of trading rules to the market and running them forward to the present to see how they performed. I learned that if I made *these* trades based on *these* quantified rules, then I would have had X result. I refined these systems, changing parameters and backtesting them again and again, figuring out through trial and error what made a positive difference in my results. If a system that I built made money in certain market conditions in the past, then I could reasonably expect it to make money during similar market conditions in the future.

This process was all-consuming for years, a huge amount of effort. I worked at it seven days a week, laboring late into the evening and on weekends and spending more than $500,000 on programmers. I continued to develop rules-based trading systems, each of which was designed to perform well in different market conditions. In 2007 I started trading using these algorithms, and this approach has served me incredibly well through all market conditions. If you apply the principles I teach in this book, you have the benefit of what I learned without all the sweat and expense.

At first, I only traded two types of systems: one that did well in rising markets, and one that did well in falling markets. There were certainly bumps along the way. For example, I traded mean reversion systems, and sometimes the market didn't provide enough volatility for them to work well. After a few years, I experienced a drawdown in one system that was much greater than my backtesting had predicted. This taught me two lessons; first, backtesting is not a foolproof way to predict performance, including drawdowns. Second, I needed more noncorrelated systems. The more of them I added in, the smoother my equity curve would become and the more consistently I would make money regardless of market conditions. Also, the more robust the combination of systems is, the less chance there is that a corporate event in one stock in which I have a large concentration will negatively impact my portfolio.

Turn Off Your TV

The best thing I discovered as I learned to trade this way was that I could—and should—ignore the financial media.

There's a huge ecosystem of television and online "experts" and publications that are in the business of getting you excited about the market. Let's be clear: they are not in the business of helping you make money. They're in the business of providing information that they think is relevant in that moment and that gathers the most clicks or views. That's how they measure success. They want you either to be afraid that you are missing out on something great or worried that something bad is about to happen. Those feelings are what keep you glued to the screen. Their business is not your financial success; their business is *their* financial success, which depends on your eyeballs.

When I understood this, I saw that the financial media had nothing at all to do with what I do as a systematic investor, and I was able to tune it out completely. That lowered the stress in my life a lot. One of the most dramatic examples of how this benefited me came during the COVID crash in March 2020. The market dropped by 33 percent, and investors panicked because there was no way to know how low it would go. This fear fed on itself in the financial media, but I didn't feel any of it. I did not experience a single day of worry about my investments because I knew I had built systems that could handle this kind of market, and I didn't need to listen to the fretting and anxiety of others. In fact, I made money that month.

Criteria for Your Success

I did not write this book for the novice investor. You're reading this book because you want better returns and more peace of mind around managing your retirement accounts. I assume that you are already a stock trader and comfortable trading, and that you are at least familiar with quantitative trading and the statistics underpinning it. You will find trading terms in here that should be familiar to you (if they are not, you can find definitions at Investopedia). If you have not read my other books, I encourage you to read at least one if you want to take a deeper dive into your emotional biases as you build systems, the mechanics of building trading systems, and the power of noncorrelated systematic trading. (*Automated Stock Trading Systems* is the most complete of the two.)

My approach will not get you rich overnight. It is not based on tricks or secrets, and I don't promise you a particular result. Success demands work and discipline, especially up front.

If what I teach were easy, everyone would do it, but not everyone does. I do know from my own experience, and that of my students, that what I teach works. I am showing you a philosophy and strategy that can address your pain points around investing your retirement account. Traders who do well with this approach consistently apply their systems. Let me say that again: *traders who do well with this approach consistently apply their systems.* Being consistent means trusting what you have built, not trading on emotion.

You might wonder why I bother to teach and write books at all. I enjoy teaching, and it makes me a better trader. My students are bright and often very experienced traders, and their questions open my eyes to things I had not considered before. They make me a better teacher and a better trader.

I wrote *The 30-Minute Stock Trader* because it was the book I wished I had available when I began to educate myself about trading. *Automated Stock Trading* built on that by unpacking the power of noncorrelated trading. *Trading Retirement Accounts* shows you how to use these principles within the constraints that are placed on trading retirement accounts so you can outperform bull and sideways markets, protect yourself during bear markets, and hedge against inflation.

Mark Twain observed that "history does not repeat itself, but it rhymes." By building and testing automated trading systems against the market data now available to you, you can develop trading systems you trust and believe in that will be ready to capitalize when history rhymes again.

Let me show you how.

CHAPTER 2

SYSTEMATIC TRADING FOR RETIREMENT ACCOUNTS

CAN WE BEAT THE MARKET? ABSOLUTELY AND RESOUNDINGLY, yes. Sure, the market grows over time, but it can be a rollercoaster. In case you don't remember, here are a couple of reminders:

- In April 2000, after a huge run-up that had lasted five years, the bull market bubble driven by tech optimism burst. The S&P 500 dropped 49 percent before it began to recover, and it took 86 months to return to its pre-collapse high, which is more than seven years.

- In 2007, at last, the S&P was back at new highs—only to drop again in 2008, this time by 56 percent. Recovery took more than five years.

More recently, the market collapsed 33 percent in March 2020 with the onset of the COVID lockdowns. There have been lesser, but still powerful, drops in 2011, 2015, 2018, and 2022. Riding out these drops is psychologically painful if not intolerable. Far too many investors, feeling more pain than they can accept, sell when things get bad. Then when the market starts to grow again, they fear they are missing out on something good and get back in. In other words, they end up selling low and buying high. This is not a recipe for success or for peace of mind.

The baseline we're competing against is the S&P 500, broadly understood as "the market." For the last twenty years, the S&P 500 has had an average compound annual growth rate of about 8 percent and a maximum drawdown (in 2008) of 56 percent. We compare the systems we build against that performance, which is what a buy-and-hold investor would have received if they had bought and held the SPY (the index fund of the S&P 500) during that time.

In the coming chapters, I will show you how to develop and combine seven separate trading systems that have different strengths and weaknesses. (The last chapter is an introduction to building trading systems.) There is no magic to seven systems; I am showing you that many to illustrate seven complementary strategies. A governing principle of my approach is that no equity trading system makes money all the time in all market conditions. Every system makes money in certain conditions and loses money in other conditions. For instance, a buy-and-hold approach is a kind of stock trading system. It makes money when the S&P 500 is rising and loses money when it is falling.

There is nothing magical about building systems. We start with one, look at the backtest results, and see where it is losing money. Then we try to develop another that makes money when the first one is losing money, and so on. This additive approach smooths the equity curve.

How Systems Combine

Let's begin with a combination of two trend following systems on stocks that do very well, but both have a drawdown during the bear markets during 2008, 2022, and the COVID crash.

Long-Term Trend Following Systems A and B Combined

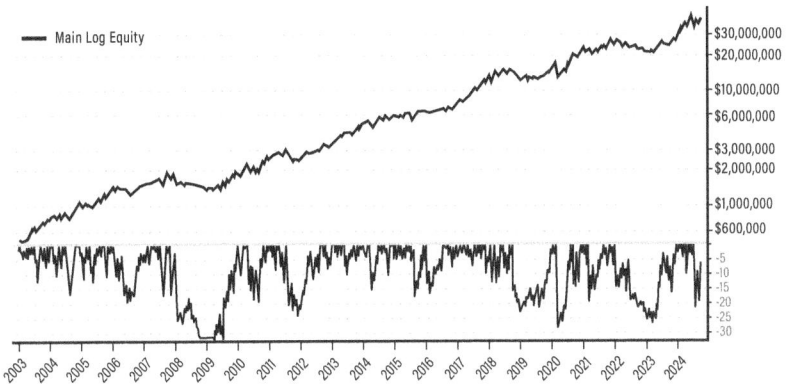

Here's how Systems A and B combined perform:

- Compound annual growth rate (CAGR): 19.9 percent
- Maximum drawdown: 33 percent
- Longest drawdown in months: 32
- MAR: 0.60

Now let's add a completely diversified strategy to this, which has the odds to make money during Systems A and B's drawdowns as it is designed to enter into completely different, noncorrelating instruments like gold, oil, agriculture, energy, and other commodities.

System C: Diversified Instruments

Here's how System C performs:

- CAGR: 5.1 percent
- Maximum drawdown: 29.5 percent
- Longest drawdown in months: 125
- MAR: 0.17

At first glance you might be inclined to discard System C because the CAGR is only 5 percent and the drawdown duration is more than 125 months. But pay attention *when* it makes money! Take a look at the same chart where I highlight this:

System B: Noncorrelated Instruments (Highlighted)

Do you see how in 2008, especially during the first part of the bear market, this strategy made money? The same happened when the big inflation jump came; in 2022 it made money too. These are exactly the pain points of Systems A and B.

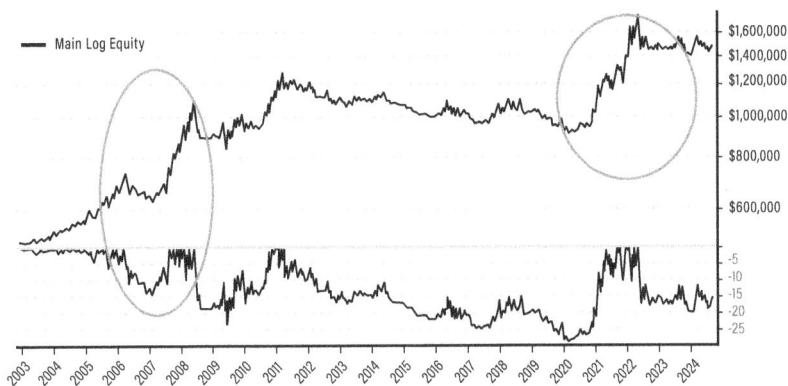

This is the kind of thing to look for as you build your suite of systems. I looked at the pain points of Systems A and B, which had a great CAGR but also a large drawdown, and developed something that is designed to attack those pain points. I call pain points potholes, and it is our task to fill those potholes, making our overall strategy more robust with more systems that cumulatively generate a lower drawdown and higher risk-adjusted return.

If we combine the three systems A, B and C, with 33.33 percent of equity devoted to each of them, here's how they perform (see the next page).

Systems A, B, and C Combined Performance

Look at the numbers and be pleasantly surprised!

	Systems A and B: Trend Following on Equities	System C: Diversified Instruments	Combined Trend Following 66.6% and Diversified Instruments 33.3%	Difference
CAGR	19.9%	5.1	18.2%	1.7% lower CAGR
Max Drawdown	33%	29.6%	22.6%	11.4% lower drawdown
Longest Drawdown	32 months	125 months	23 months	9 months shorter drawdown
MAR	0.6	0.17	0.81	0.21 higher MAR

You are trading a 2 percent drop in CAGR to reduce your drawdown by 11.4 percent and your drawdown duration by nine months. That's a great tradeoff because you reduce your time and depth underwater (when you are catching up to an earlier high). This is 100 percent worth it.

Every time we look at our equity curve, we see what we have, see where the pain (pothole) is, and then look for a strategy that is conceptually designed to fill that hole. That's how we achieve the objective of lowering drawdowns and increasing the risk-adjusted return.

Keep It Simple

Every system has ten ingredients, and it's important to keep them simple so you don't overoptimize (more on this problem below):

1. Trading universe
2. Filters
3. Setup
4. Ranking
5. Entry
6. Stop-loss
7. Re-entry
8. Profit protection
9. Profit taking
10. Position sizing

All our systems have a statistical edge so that over time they will make more money than they lose, and when some systems are losing money, others are making money. For instance, let's imagine you are trading only two systems, with your $100,000 equity split evenly between them. The first is a long-term trend following system that will do well in a long bull market. You might be up 30 percent ($15,000) in a year to $65,000. But then the market turns down 25 percent, your positions are stopped out, and you take a 20 percent ($13,000) loss on that system. You're still up by 4 percent ($2,000) on your initial investment of $50,000. (I have simplified the math for purposes of this example.)

Meanwhile, imagine that you're trading another system that invests the other half of your equity only in a portfolio of very uncorrelated stocks and doesn't closely track the broader market. This system goes up 15 percent ($7,500) to a total of $57,500 as the broader market is dropping.

So where do you stand at the end of the year? You started with $100,000 and now have $109,500. Meanwhile, if someone had simply invested $100,000 at the beginning of the year in the S&P 500 index (SPY), they are down 25 percent overall and stand at $75,000. You did 34.5 percent better than the market.

That's the power of combining systems. The complementary nature of different systems—the way they help each other—is far more important than the power of any individual system.

Trading a suite of complementary systems works, but there are some hard things about it. Perhaps the hardest is sticking to your systems. I'll get more into building your own systems in the last chapter, but you might already be asking yourself, **why should I build my own when I could just copy yours? Because we are different. You do not**

see the world the way I see it. You do not have my objectives. You do not have my philosophy about the market. You do not have my risk tolerance. This is true for all of us. Building your own systems, rooted in your own values and beliefs and developed on your own, is the best path to creating systems that you understand and trust.

What is foundational is that you embrace the philosophy of combining different systems that make and lose money differently so that you can be confident that you will do better than the market regardless of market conditions. We all want to make money, protect our capital during bear markets, and be insulated against the effects of inflation, but there are many roads on the way to Rome. In this book I give you a step-by-step blueprint of how to build a set of systems that accomplish this. Your systems will not be my systems; this book is an example of approaches that you can follow as you find your own path.

This is incredibly important because there will come times when your systems lose money and the urge to suspend them—to go to cash and stop trading—will be strong. An antidote to this is to understand why your systems are losing money. They may be losing money for exactly the right reasons—because you built them to lose money in these particular market conditions, knowing that they make money in other conditions. As soon as you suspend, you are trying to time the market, and that never works.

You can build a great, robust system, and it could still lose money for years. Imagine you launched a long-term trend following term in early 2009. You would make money for years as the market climbed out of the 2008 financial crisis. Now imagine you launched that system in late 2007. You'd lose money and go into a significant drawdown. If you suspended it in 2008, you then missed the big run-up that followed. There was nothing wrong with the system in 2008; it was the same one that started making money in 2009. It's just that your timeframe and the system's short-term performance changed. Consequently, I tell traders they should plan on trading a system for at least two years before they evaluate it. **In order to get the results that I show in this book, and that your backtests will project for you, you must consistently execute trading your systems without doubt.**

The second major risk traders face is anchoring expectations to projections. Imagine that you develop a system that you project to generate CAGR of 20 percent. You begin trading it and expect it to make 20 percent, and it makes 22 percent the first year. Brilliant! You're feeling good about it. The second year, though, it only returns 6 percent. How are you feeling about it now? The third year it returns 33 percent. Now how are you feeling?

I'll give you a hint—you should feel neutral every year. Over three years, that system returned an average 20 percent CAGR to you, just as you projected that it would. As you'll see in the coming pages, the systems we build deliver a wide range of returns. The CAGR is an average, and it's easy to forget that. I have learned to neither get excited nor disappointed by any one year's results on a system if it's performing conceptually the way I expect it to perform.

Emotional neutrality is very important in this kind of trading. You are not looking to ride any sort of market wave, to time the market, to get in on the next big thing. In fact, if you go on a strict financial news media diet, you may not even know what the market is doing outside of what you see on your trading screen. Good! We maintain neutrality by building and backtesting systems when we are feeling emotionally neutral. Often, traders "paper trade" a system for months, testing it in the live market as if they were trading real money. When you start to trade, trust your computer. Your job is to execute the trades it tells you to trade every day without question. The computer has no emotion—that gives you a huge edge over other traders and should give you great peace of mind. You can trade without emotion because you are dealing with an emotionless machine that is trading an algorithm that you developed calmly and methodically and that you trust, regardless of the daily fluctuations. It's really a very pleasant state of mind.

Backtests Are the Backbone of Systematic Trading

When we create a system, we backtest it against historical market data. This process has its limits, for it can only tell us about the past. Nevertheless, the past can teach us a lot about what's likely to happen and how to profit from it.

I conducted all the backtests for the systems in this book using a historical dataset from 2003 to September 30, 2024. (I get my data from Norgate Data because you need high-quality data to create a reasonable representation of the past. In my experience, Norgate Data does a good job.)

I don't backtest farther than 2003 because some of my systems trade exchange-traded funds (ETFs), and data for them only goes back to roughly 2003. The dataset I use captures a variety of market conditions and scenarios, which we want. The more market conditions we can capture, the more insight we can gain from backtest results.

I use end-of-day data that includes the opening price, daily high, daily low, closing price, volume, and adjusted close and that takes into account stock splits and dividends. The database includes more than forty thousand stocks, about half of which are delisted. We included delisted stocks because we should backtest on as complete a picture of past reality as we can. When companies fail, exchanges remove them from their listings. If you backtest only on the remaining stocks, the survivorship bias will skew to a much better performance for your long-term trend following systems than would have happened in reality.

To be conservative in my predictions, I exclude interest earned on my cash balance. In the past, this interest often was negligible, but higher rates in recent years have brought better returns for cash. Some of the systems I describe may have very high cash positions—even 100 percent at times—but I don't count the interest when calculating equity.

Commission payments must be part of your calculations. I build into my systems the same commissions that I pay at my brokerage, Interactive Brokers, plus a very conservative slippage calculation (the difference between the expected price of a trade and the actual price).

Beware Over-Optimization

What makes a suite of trading systems work is having clear, complementary objectives for each system. For each system, ask yourself:

- When is it supposed to make money?
- When is it supposed to lose money?

Some investors struggle with the second question because they are very loss averse. The pain of losing money is much greater than the pleasure of making money, and this can be especially true when dealing with retirement accounts. Because of that internal psychological pressure, they can succumb to the trap of over-optimizing their systems. Yet understanding when your system is most likely not to perform well is even more important than understanding when it will make money. When it's making money, you're not at risk of doubting yourself and shutting it down. It's only when a system is losing money that you face that risk. Periods of nonperformance are periods when you run the risk of suspending the system or, worse, running behind the facts and pursuing some other system that did well recently.

Is systematic trading an art or a science?

It is the art of applying the science correctly. If you overoptimize, you are not applying the science correctly.

Let me explain. Many of the trading programs available to investors today have some version of an "Optimize" button. I try to teach my students to see this as the "Abuse" button because if you use it, you are abusing the power of the computer—the science of building trading systems—to make your backtested results look better than they should. In simplest terms, over-optimizing means filtering out the bad results and overemphasizing the good results. That's not what you intend to do, but that's what's happening inside your system. The future, however, will not lend itself to such selective trading. You will of course have bad trades in your system, many more than an over-optimized system predicts on backtests, leading to mistrust and disappointment. With the huge computing power available these days, it is very easy to abuse the historical data and simulations by hugely optimizing a system, creating something that looks great on paper but is useless in live trading.

I will discuss building systems briefly at the end of the book, but the risks of over-optimization are so great that I want to highlight them here.

We think of the word *optimize* in a positive sense because it means making things as good as they can be. The art of building robust systems is understanding when you are making them *too* good. Remember a fundamental concept of how we build quantitative trading systems: backtesting systems against past market data to gain insight into the likely future behavior of those systems. The weak link here is that the only data we have available is past data, and the future will not be like the past. It's an echo or a rhyme, not a replica. When you backtest, you can fit your system to the data—that is, continue to optimize it to find the very best result from that past dataset. But the past dataset will not be the future dataset, and you will not get the same result in the future.

There are several ways to ensure we are not over-optimizing. The first is to look for conceptually correct results. I had a student build a long-term trend following system that, when backtested, lost almost nothing during the 2008 financial crisis. This was not a conceptually correct system; he had found a set of parameters that happened to select just the right individual stocks and trades to avoid that market meltdown. There is no way to build a system that would operate like that in the future, and if he traded this system, he would have seen much worse performance in real life. If you are building a long-term trend following (LTTF) system, look for it to make money in bull markets and lose money during bear periods. A mean reversion system should make money in sideways volatile markets, and so on.

Another red flag for over-optimization is having too many indicators for your system. If you have a series of filters or a complex setup, what you are doing is driving your system toward mining the data. Don't do it. If you have five different rules in place to set up a trade, that's probably too many. Don't stack a large combination of fancy rules that backtest well in periods where they really should not have, because you are just fooling yourself. The chance of replicating your results in live trading goes down with complexity. Try to make your system as simple as you can and still achieve your objectives.

One way I like to avoid over-optimizing is to chart multiple results by varying one factor in my systems, then looking for the middle of the performance curve to ensure robustness. For example, if an entry rule to buy above the 200-day simple moving average tests well, then 180, 190, 210, and 220 days should all produce fairly similar results. Don't cherry pick the best number.

Try to build systems that have a single market filter, single trend filter, and single ranking system. To simulate over-optimization, add another market or trend filter. In all likelihood you will reduce your maximum drawdown substantially, but you also sharply reduce the likelihood that you are modeling future behavior of the system. It's much more likely that you are data mining.

Adopt this mindset: When you build a system, look for it to lose money in the wrong market conditions just as much as you look for it to make money in the right market conditions.

Position Sizing

Position sizing is a way of managing risk. In my second book, I laid out how to use position size and percent risk in combination to limit the risk of any single trade. This is a very important concept and one that I encourage you to explore separately. For the purposes of this book, I have adopted a very simple position sizing model, and it's the same for each system:

- A maximum of ten stocks can be held by each system.

- Invest 10 percent of the system's equity in each stock.

- So, if we have a $10,000 account, we can have a maximum of $10,000 per position.

- If we have six open positions (6 x $10,000 = $60,000), we can only place a maximum of four more orders.

This design is sufficient for the purpose of teaching you the concepts behind each of the systems. For the moment, don't get caught up in position sizing. When you build your own systems, use an appropriate sizing algorithm to limit your per-trade risk. If you would like to learn more about position sizing, please refer to my first two books. The focus of this book is to show you how to combine systems to grow your wealth in bull markets, protect it in bear markets, and hedge against inflation.

CHAPTER 3

OUR INVESTING APPROACH: TREND FOLLOWING AND MEAN REVERSION

BECAUSE OF THE RULES AROUND RETIREMENT ACCOUNTS, WE limit our approach to two basic styles of trading: Long-term trend following long and mean reversion (MR) long. Philosophically, these take two different approaches to the market.

LTTF long systems invest in the generally bullish tendency of the market, banking on the fact that stocks tend to rise over time and looking for opportunities within that general trend. To gain an edge, we use market filters and trend filters to find stocks that are on the rise in a rising market. Once we find a stock that meets our criteria, we buy and hold it for as long as it is going up. We don't sell right at the peak because it's impossible to know where that peak is. Instead, we set a trailing stop loss that protects some of our profit, accepting that we will give some profit back to ensure that we are selling only when the stock truly has ended its bull run. LTTF systems make money over a long time, potentially a great deal on single trades.

An Ideal LTTF Trade

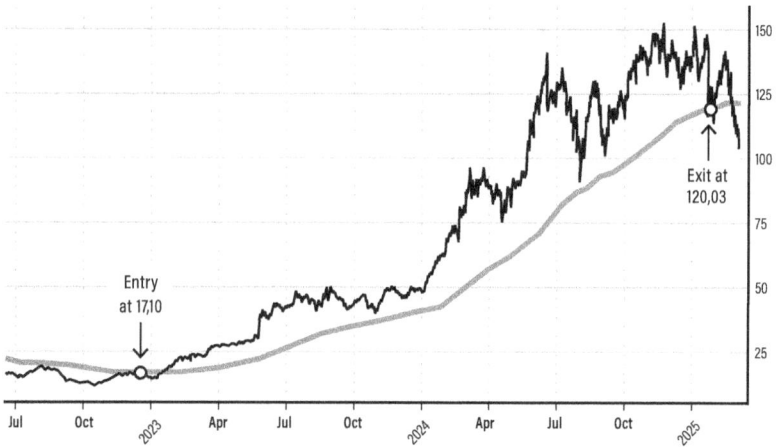

The core concept behind a trend following trade is to cut your losses and let your profits run. What you're hunting for with trend following is outliers like the big Tesla long trade or the big Nvidia long trade. These are rare bull elephants, but when you come up, you get in and stay in, riding them as long as you can until the return curve definitively bends down. In this scenario, for trend following systems, **the unknown of a big upside is your friend**. With an appropriate trailing stop and a long rising trend, a single trade can be enormously profitable.

MR long systems, on the other hand, look for short-lived deviations from a stock's trading range. With MR long systems (the only kind we can trade in retirement accounts), we buy fear and sell greed. That is, we buy stocks that have been temporarily oversold, then quickly sell as soon as they begin to move back up toward their mean price. (MR short systems buy greed and sell fear.) Stocks that are volatile, or that can be knocked down by bad news, are good candidates for mean reversion. MR systems are designed to make a little money over short periods of time but do so frequently.

An Ideal MR Long Trade

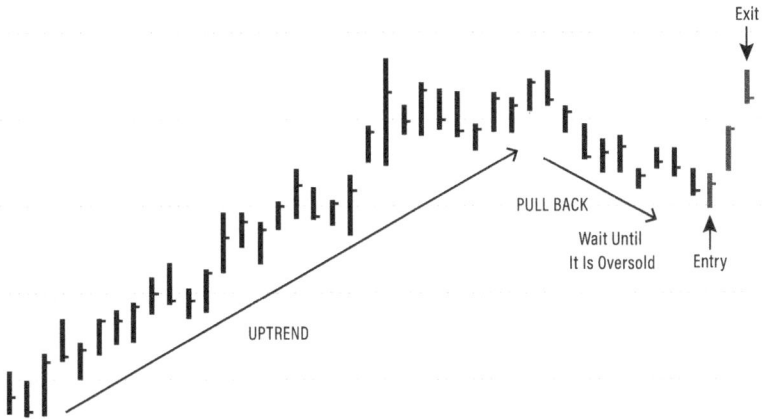

The philosophy of mean reversions is that the unknown is your enemy. With mean reversion, rather than seeking a single big elephant to ride to riches, we are looking to pile up many quick, small trades that yield a good return over time. The unknown downside is your enemy, which is why we get out of mean reversion trades quickly.

Some people like to trade only one style of system, such as long-term trend following. LTTF systems have a low trade frequency and are philosophically oriented to a generally bullish approach. They also are useful if you're trading a taxable account in which you want to generate only long-term gains, which have a lower federal tax rate. Temperamentally, that's where some investors are most comfortable, and that's fine. Your systems will outperform bull markets but will go into larger drawdowns than mean reversion systems do.

The Tools We Have

In order to accumulate our wealth in bull and sideways markets and to preserve our wealth in bear markets, we can use the following approaches:

- **The use of stop-loss mechanisms on our trades.** This will eventually result in your systems being in cash and in most cases will save you from the most painful losses. Imagine a scenario like the 1929–1932 Great Depression, where the markets plummeted more than 85 percent, or the crisis in 2008, where the maximum drawdown of the S&P 500 was 56 percent. You might lose 20 or 25 percent before your stop losses kick in, but that's far better than holding on for the ride. Cash was a pretty good place to be!

- **Spread your trading equity across different types of systems**, some of which are designed to not even be in the market when the markets start to decline. This further reduces your downside risk and preserves capital.

- **Diversify into ETFs in a basket of commodities and other noncorrelated asset classes** that can help you to actually *make* money in declining markets. Most important, these must be assets that have little correlation to the broader stock market. Think here of asset classes like metals, energy, agriculture, or other stocks that have a low correlation to the broader market.

- **Diversify among the style of strategies**. Trend following behaves very differently than mean reversion, our two primary strategies.

- **Diversify by using different time frames in your lookbacks** as your systems evaluate candidate stocks for investment.

- **Use long-duration and short-duration strategies**. This means strategies that are designed to have a long trade duration, capitalize hugely on big bull markets, and use strategies that are only in the market for one, two, or three days.

- **Have strategies that trade in loosely correlated sectors** to offer additional diversification, called sector diversification.

- **For some systems, use an exit strategy that gets out of the market during downturns** and stays on the sidelines until there are clear upturn signals.

As part of the fifty-five systems that I personally trade, I run a dozen trend following systems, and I improve their noncorrelation by limiting some of them to trading within certain sectors like biotech, healthcare, aerospace, energy, and real estate. You can trade in many sectors to diversify your investments. If you only want to use a trend following strategy, you can look for ways like this to diversify and reduce your correlation. These sectors are loosely correlated to the broader market, so this approach will far outperform a buy-and-hold approach. (Of course, if you bring in mean reversion, you'll do even better.)

Having said all that, there are no guarantees in trading. Here are a few ironclad rules to remember:

- The future is not the past. Your systems will not mimic your backtest results.

- Expect drawdowns to be bigger than your backtest predicts.

- Sometimes, everything correlates despite our best efforts. Often in a panic sell-off, and when facing the disadvantage of trading long only in all stocks and sectors, you can have a short period of time where all your assets are correlated. This is where your stop losses and your very short lookbacks on certain systems (which most likely are not even in the market) will help preserve your capital.

The Results of Our Approach

Our objective is to create a suite of complementary systems that result in a smooth equity curve, one where we see steady gains regardless of market conditions. It's easier to do this when we can trade short as well as long, but even when we are limited by the rules to long trading only, we still can generate superior results.

The seven systems described in this book produce the following results when backtested for twenty-two years:

- CAGR: 20.41 percent
- Maximum drawdown: 15.81 percent
- MAR: 1.29
- Longest drawdown: 15.2 months

Our hypothetical investor who bought and held the SPY for the same twenty years made money too—but not nearly as much.

- CAGR: 8.86 percent
- Maximum drawdown: 56.7 percent
- MAR: 0.16
- Longest drawdown: 65.4 months

Let those numbers sink in for a moment. Try to truly imagine watching more than half your wealth disappear as the market sank. Would you stay invested? Could you? What would that mean for your life, for your family? Now try to imagine taking more than five years to claw your way back to just being even with where you were before that big drawdown. That's five years when you were not growing your retirement funds. What would that mean for your life and for your peace of mind?

There is nothing magical about what I am going to show you and nothing magical about how these systems perform. I simply take a different approach to investing than buy-and-hold investors. Nor is there anything magical about seven systems. I happen to trade more than fifty systems in my own accounts, the result of spending years looking for an edge. You can build other systems if they follow the principles I teach and do well with them. We get this result by building a system that works in certain marketing conditions, complementing it with another system that works in different market conditions, on so on, additively improving the combined systems' performance across a range of market conditions, reducing volatility, and improving the average CAGR and drawdowns.

Let's see how, beginning with trend following systems.

CHAPTER 4

SYSTEM #1: TREND FOLLOWING ON S&P 500 STOCKS

OUR FIRST TRADING SYSTEM IS A VERY SIMPLE TREND FOLLOW-ing system. Every system has an objective and rules. I'll lay those out and then discuss them.

Objectives are the base for each system. Without a clear objective, you'd have no idea what entry or exit rules it should have. Every objective should state the purpose of the system and when it is supposed to make money and likely to lose money. The more clearly you define this, the easier it is to find the indicators to enter and exit that help you achieve that objective.

Objective

This system needs to make money when the overall market is in a big bull market. We will be looking for longer-term trends, both for the S&P 500 and for the stock itself. We want to be in the strongest performing stocks of the S&P 500. Once we are in, we want to give these stocks some space to continue their trend and make sure that we ride the trend as long as it is trending. Once the trend is over, we exit.

This system is supposed to have a very low trade frequency with minimal maintenance.

The obvious weakness of this system is that when the trending stocks start to decline, the system starts to lose money. This is also at the same time a necessity in order to capture the big moves. It will therefore be likely to be losing money once big trends reverse and in bear markets.

Rules

- Trading universe: All stocks in the S&P 500.

- Liquidity filter: Trade only the stocks that are currently in the top 25 percent of the highest average volume over the last twenty days.

- Setup: Get into a stock if the following are all true:
  - Close of the S&P 500 index is above the 200-day simple moving average (SMA).
  - The close of the stock is higher than two hundred trading days ago.

- Ranking: If we have more than ten candidate stocks to trade, we give preference to the stocks with the highest relative strength over the last two hundred trading days.
  - Buy the next day at market price on open.

- Exit rules:
  - Once we are in a position, the next day we place a stop loss of 7 percent below the closing price.

- If the position is profitable, we use a trailing stop of 25 percent.
- If either stop is triggered, we exit the next day on the open price.

The whole idea of a system like this is to get into the strongest stocks in a bull market and stay in them until there is a reason to get out. This is a system that will have more losing trades than winning trades (about 60 percent losing trades), but the average winning trade is 7.8 times larger than the average losing trade.

We use different initial stop loss and trailing stop-loss numbers for two reasons. The initial stop loss is relatively small—7 percent—in case we have mistimed the trade and gotten into the stock just as it is losing its upward trend. If that's the case, we get stopped out fairly quickly and minimize losses. The smaller the stop loss, the more losing trades you will have.

The 25 percent trailing stop gives the stock room to run. No stock has a steady upward trend day after day; there will be days, even on a bull run, where the stock retracts. If you set your trailing stop too tightly, you may get stopped out on one of those days and miss the full length of the stock's run. A 25 percent trailing stop allows breathing room for volatility. It's the sort of parameter that can keep you in volatile growth stocks like Nvidia and Tesla.

It can be hard to give back 25 percent—we want to limit our downside. But testing has shown that setting generous trailing stops results in an improved equity curve. It is the only way to capture the extended big moves.

This is a typical framework for a long-term trend follow-ing system. There are many variations that can work well. For example, you could use a different mechanism for entry rules, such as the highest rate of change, Keltner channels, Bollinger bands, etc., or a different exit mechanism. There's no magic to these rules because there's no magic to any of our systems.

Simulated Returns of System #1, 2003–2024

- CAGR: 19.95 percent
- Maximum drawdown: 32.96 percent
- Longest drawdown in months: 32
- MAR: 0.61
- Winning trades: 32.8 percent
- Average winning vs. losing trades ratio: 7.8 to 1

System #1 Equity Curve

System #1 Yearly Return vs. Benchmark

Year	Days	End Total Equity	Total Equty Gain/Loss	# Trades	Annual Gain	Benchmark	Comparison
2003	252	$739,094.10	$239,094.10	28	47.82%	22.32%	25.50%
2004	252	$1,045,343.18	$306,249.08	28	41.44%	8.99%	32.44%
2005	252	$1,482,558.29	$437,215.11	36	41.83%	3.00%	38.82%
2006	251	$1,543,886.99	$61,328.70	44	4.14%	13.62%	-9.48%
2007	251	$1,865,036.05	$321,149.06	60	20.80%	3.53%	17.27%
2008	253	$1,558,294.41	($306,741.64)	10	-16.45%	-38.49%	22.04%
2009	252	$1,772,023.50	$213,729.09	64	13.72%	23.45%	-9.74%
2010	252	$1,940,183.58	$168,160.08	48	9.49%	12.78%	-3.29%
2011	252	$1,755,888.96	($184,294.62)	40	-9.50%	0.00%	-9.50%
2012	250	$2,552,470.92	$796,581.96	28	45.37%	13.41%	31.96%
2013	252	$4,060,176.77	$1,507,705.85	12	59.07%	29.60%	29.47%
2014	252	$5,004,734.59	$944,557.83	16	23.26%	11.39%	11.87%
2015	252	$5,358,085.00	$353,350.41	26	7.06%	-0.73%	7.79%
2016	252	$6,220,711.13	$862,626.13	36	16.10%	9.54%	6.56%
2017	251	$9,471,076.62	$3,250,365.49	14	52.25%	19.42%	32.83%
2018	251	S8,692,429.58	($778,647.05)	35	-8.22%	-6.24%	-1.98%
2019	252	$10,224,482.86	$1,532,053.29	27	17.63%	28.88%	-11.25%
2020	253	$11,777,406.25	$1,552,923.39	22	15.19%	16.26%	-1.07%
2021	252	$15,754,668.50	$3,977,262.25	22	33.77%	26.89%	6.88%
2022	251	$14,674,465.24	($1,080,203.25)	32	-6.86%	-19.44%	12.59%
2023	250	$16,574,560.79	$1,900,095.54	44	12.95%	24.23%	-11.28%
2024	185	$25,741,885.26	$9,167,324.47	18	55.31%	19.97%	35.34%

When we look at the annual returns, remember what we're looking for. Not only do we want to see the system making money in bull markets, we want to see it losing money in bear markets.

In the big bull years of 2003, 2013, 2019, 2023, and 2024, the system makes money. Notice, though, that it doesn't always outperform the benchmark. Take 2023 as an example. Our system made almost 13 percent, but it underperformed the larger market by almost 12 percent. Why would that be? Look at the previous year, which was a bear year—the market as a whole lost more than 19 percent. But our system lost less than 7 percent. Why? Because for the most part we were on the sidelines. If the system is stopped out on your positions and market conditions are not bullish, there will not be investment opportunities. Now, with the system on the sidelines, the market turned up in 2023.

Look at our entry rules: the market has to be above the 200-day SMA before the system will look for candidate stocks. That means the bull market is well underway before we get in. We miss out on some of the early gains in the market and thus underperform the market as a whole. That's part of the price you pay to make sure the market is bullish before getting in.

But once we're in, as the market continues to grow, our system begins to outperform the index. In 2024 the system beat the S&P 500 by more than 35 percent.

Even more important than accepting that you will be late into bull markets is accepting possible large drawdowns. Almost all of us have a powerful sense of loss aversion; we hate losing something even more than we like getting something. In 2008, the benchmark was down 38 percent, and our system was down more than 16 percent. Comparitively, we did well, but that's still a significant drawdown. It's essential to remember that this is normal. If you develop an LTTF system that makes money in bear markets during backtesting, you have over-optimized it.

If the market drops 30 percent or 50 percent, you are going to lose money, and that's okay. The trailing stop losses almost always limit the potential downside. That's why in 2008 our system's drop was less than half of the S&P 500 drop. We see the same thing in 2022, when our system dropped only one-third as much as the broader index.

Keep one important caveat in mind, however. A trailing stop works well if a stock goes through a relatively moderate decline over time. There can be situations where a stock will open sharply lower than the previous day's close, called "gapping down." Often this is the result of some sort of news event. For instance, a biotech company may report after hours that its promising new drug did not get government approval, or a CEO may be accused of fraud. In situations like that, the stock may gap down from its close. It might close at 50 and open at 30. Your 25 percent trailing stop loss will not limit your losses at that point. Yes, you will get out of the stock, but you will get out at the market price, far lower than the stop-loss price. This is one reason why we have to remember that backtested results do not predict the future; at best they are an indication of what you could expect. Eventually, the maximum drawdown you experience during backtesting may be smaller than the maximum drawdown you experience in live trading. Professional systematic traders that I know who manage over a billion dollars and have a great track record all say the same thing: **Your largest drawdown is always in the future.** That's all the more reason why we want multiple, diverse trading systems— spread your eggs across multiple baskets.

Historically, equity markets have an average CAGR of about 8 percent. Equities are generally bullish but not always. As you backtest, it's important not to fall into the trap of thinking that what you see in a backtest from 2003 to 2024 is a good representation of how your systems will perform. That was an unusually bullish period in history, so let's look farther back—all the way to 1960. That allows us to test against the 2000 dot com crash, the 1987 crash, and the inflationary period from the mid-1960s to the mid-1980s. This period is particularly interesting because the market as a whole was essentially flat for sixteen years! If you factor in inflation, it actually fell about 70 percent. What a terrible time for a buy-and-hold strategy. Going back to 1960, we encompass a broader range of market conditions and can see how the system performs with its rules in those conditions.

System #1 Results Simulation, 1960–2024

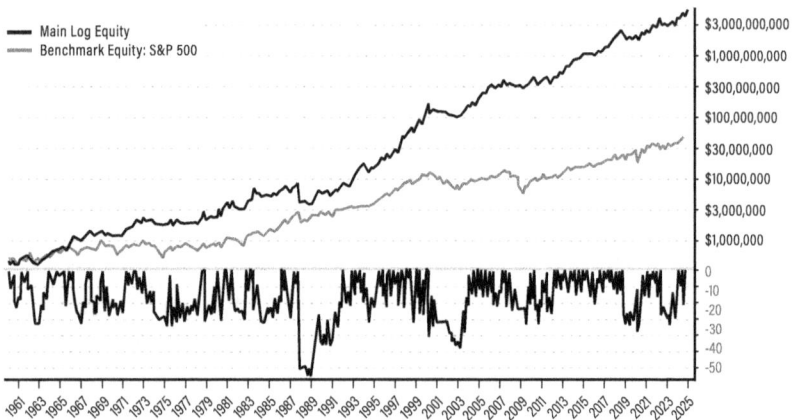

Simulated Returns of System #1, 1960–2024

- CAGR: 15.3 percent
- Maximum drawdown: 58 percent

The drop in CAGR makes sense since the earlier markets were less bullish than they have been in the last two decades, yet the system still achieved double the benchmark CAGR. From 1964 to 1982, it averaged 11 percent per year, while the benchmark averaged 2.7 percent per year. The big drawdown comes in the 1987 crash, and it's much larger than the 20 percent decline the market as a whole experienced. This is because the system was invested in more volatile stocks than the market as a whole.

Also, remember the way that crash happened—it was very sudden. This was a situation where some stocks gapped down overnight and opened outside the stop-loss limit, as I described above. The system exited the stock with greater losses than the stop-loss amount.

What I want you to learn from this exercise is that whatever your backtests show, you will get an idea of the performance you can expect but not a guarantee. In fact, I encourage you to look at the results of backtests as evidence of what you *cannot* expect. The backtests deliver specific results down to the one-hundredth decimal point of a percent return—that specificity is misleading. In my experience, anytime I or one of my student live trades a system, eventually we see a larger drawdown than we have predicted. Expect that from the beginning and you'll be much happier.

Our LTTF System #1 reliably makes money in bull markets and loses it in bear markets. Let's turn our attention to a second system that performs differently so that we can begin to smooth out our equity curve.

CHAPTER 5

SYSTEM #2: LONG-TERM TREND FOLLOWING ON NASDAQ 100 STOCKS

NOW THAT WE HAVE A SYSTEM WITH ONE SET OF RULES, LET'S build one with a different set.

Objective

We want to diversify by the stock universe; instead of focusing on the broad market, we focus here on tech stocks. The main objective is to be in different stocks in a different sector. We want to diversify by entry frequency. In the previous system, the lookback for the trend was two hundred days; here we use one hundred days, which gets us in earlier.

We aim to avoid getting into the same stocks, and therefore we have a very different ranking. Here we give priority to the ten stocks with the highest dollar volume.

We want to make sure that we have a different exit mechanism. If we were to use the same exit rules (stop loss and trailing stop) we could expect that the market structure treats System #1 and System #2 the same, and that increases the risk that both systems underperform at the same time.

We can still expect some overlap of returns in strong bull years and bear years.

Rules

- Trading universe: All stocks of the NASDAQ 100.

- Entry rules
  - Close of the NQ100 index is above the hundred-day exponential moving average.
  - The close of the stock is above the hundred-day Keltner channel plus 2 ATR (average true range).
  - If we have more than ten candidates to trade, we give preference to the stocks with the average highest dollar volume of the last hundred days.
  - Buy the next day on market on open.

- Exit rules
  - If the close is below the hundred-day Keltner channel minus 1 ATR (twenty-one-day lookback), we exit the stock the next day at market price on open.

The NASDAQ 100 is a different index than the S&P 500, but many stocks will be in both indices, which is why it's important to have different lookbacks, entry rules, and rankings. Otherwise, you run the risk of entering the same stocks you have bought in System #1, and that contradicts our overall objective of creating diverse, noncorrelated systems.

Our lookback is one hundred days, rather than two hundred days for System #1, and we're using a different measurement (Keltner channel plus 2 ATR). Then, by giving preference to stocks with the highest average dollar volume over the last one hundred days, we are getting into the most liquid stocks in the NASDAQ 100 at a time when both the stocks and the market are trending up over the last one hundred days. This is a significantly different filter than System #1, in which we were seeking stocks with the highest relative strength after a two-hundred-day bull run.

Because we're seeking the stocks with the biggest volume, we're going to be in stocks that have heavy institutional involvement. These are often the market leaders.

Just as our entry rules are different, so are the exit rules. Rather than using a stop loss and a trailing stop, we use a single rule: exit if the stock is below the hundred-day Keltner channel minus 1 ATR. The entry was above the 100-day Keltner channel plus 2 ATR. In total, that's a range of 3 ATR from the entry point to the exit point. That rule functions like a stop loss and a trailing stop. As the stock moves up, the Keltner channel (which is an exponential moving average) will start to trail the price, but because it's an exponential moving average it will give more weight to recent data and move up with the stock. We stay in the stock as long as it is above the 100-day Keltner channel minus 1 ATR, then get out on open the next day.

Results

- CAGR: 23.8 percent
- Maximum drawdown: 41.3 percent
- Longest drawdown in months: 25
- MAR: 0.58

- Winning trades: 46.4 percent
- Average winning vs. losing trades ratio: 4.93

These results make sense when we keep in mind that the NASDAQ is more volatile than the S&P 500. We get a better CAGR than System #1 but also a larger maximum drawdown.

System #2 Equity Curve

The CAGR is almost three times the benchmark return, but this comes at a cost: big drawdowns.

It's crucial to understand that for trend following systems to achieve high compound annual growth rates, you must accept large drawdowns.

Plus, when you are in the NASDAQ, which can be more volatile than other trading universes, drawdowns can be large. Giving back some profits is part of trend following.

You see this in 2008 and 2022. Then the system makes a lot of money in 2023 and 2024, which were big bull markets.

What's most important is what happens when we combine systems. The first column in the table below shows the results of System #1, the second of System #2. The third column shows what happens if we combine both systems by dividing assets equally between them. Now we have a CAGR almost as good as the System #2 CAGR and a maximum drawdown almost as good as in System #1. This is because the drawdowns happen at different times, and that's one of the indicators of noncorrelation.

This is only the beginning of the results we will see as we add more systems. We are aiming to smooth the equity curve, which will be represented by a higher and higher MAR number. I said above that there is no magic to what we do in systematic trading, but this kind of combination can seem magical.

Results of Combining Systems #1 and #2

	S&P 500 Trend Following	NASDAQ 100 Trend Following	Combined 50% each
CAGR	19.9%	23.8%	22.9%
Max Drawdown	32.9%	41.3%	32.5%
MAR	0.61	0.58	0.70

Both systems are designed to make money in bull markets and lose it in bear markets, and both are long-term trend following systems, but they operate in different ways. In one, we get into the highest-performing stocks of the S&P 500. In the other, we get into the most liquid stocks of the NASDAQ. We look back over different time periods. All of this creates diversification.

But as you can see on the next chart, it's not that much diversification. There is still a lot of correlation between the two systems, although you can also see some differences, such as when the S&P system declines in 2010 while the NASDAQ system stayed mostly flat and then climbed sharply. On the other hand, during the COVID crash of March 2020, they both dropped sharply—as did almost everything. Sometimes, during extreme moments, noncorrelated systems will correlate.

Equity Curve for System #1 and System #2

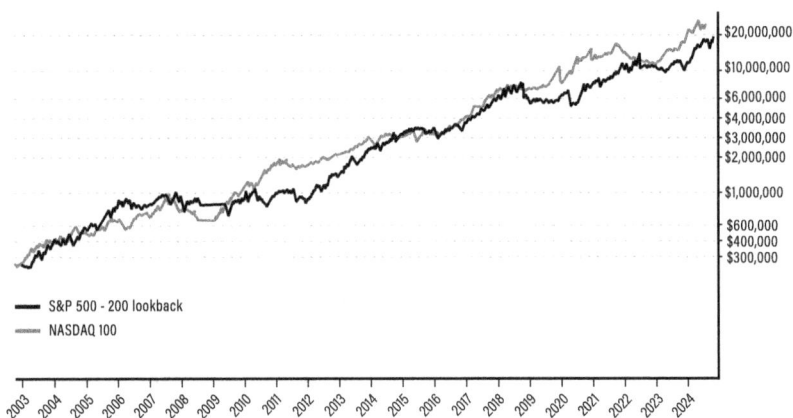

They're both trend following and both broadly invested in equities, so while we're starting to see diversification, it's not sufficient. Let's bring in another system.

CHAPTER 6

SYSTEM #3: INFLATION HEDGE

CAGR can be a distraction. It's almost like candy for investors; we all want the highest possible CAGR. Of course, high returns come with high risk, and in our systems, that translates to big drawdowns. That's why I like to focus on MAR, which is the ratio of CAGR divided by maximum percent drawdown (CAGR percent / Maximum drawdown percent). There are many other more sophisticated statistical measurements that measure risk-adjusted returns, possibly more useful than MAR, but for this book and its purpose, I want to keep it simple and focus on something that intuitively makes a lot of sense.

I consistently see investors minimize the psychological impact of a big drawdown. They are attracted to the projected CAGR, and they tell themselves that the drawdowns won't bother them that much. But they do bother them. Most investors tell themselves they can handle a drawdown of 20 or 30 percent without worrying, but in my experience they bail out and suspend their systems from trading because the psychological pain is too high. Whatever you think is an acceptable drawdown, you're probably fooling yourself. Cut your estimate in half and you may be closer to the truth of what you can live with.

In practice, this means trimming your expectations of CAGR. You'll be building a more conservative system and, critically, one that you are likely to keep trading through the drawdowns. That's important for your long-term return. In the same way that you can't catch fish if you don't have a line in the water, you can't make money if you're not trading your systems. Once you build systems that can make money in almost all market conditions, you'll have a lot more peace of mind about staying in the market even during drawdowns.

Objective

Create a system that is designed to diversify with instruments that are not correlated to the broader equity markets, has a large chance of doing exceptionally well during inflationary times, and has no corporate risk.

This system is designed to fill the gap at times when other more conventional equity long systems all lose money. It also is designed to offer diversification by instruments, which can be crucial in times when equity markets do not do well. It is supposed to make money when commodity prices increase in value and aims to not give back too much money when commodity markets are declining.

Rules

- Trading universe: Exchange traded funds (ETFs) that follow asset classes such as the following:
  - GLD (SPDR Gold Shares)
  - USO (United States Oil Fund LP)
  - DBA (Invesco DB Agriculture Fund)

- DBC (Invesco DB Commodity Index Tracking Fund)
- XLE (Energy Select Sector SPDR Fund)

Here are a couple of important notes on this portfolio:

- ETFs are a derivative of the spot prices of these markets and therefore move a bit differently than the commodities themselves.

- This is just a sample portfolio that is decently diversified. I highly recommend you not limit yourself to these ETFs as there are many more ETFs out there that could offer even more diversification. Look at the instruments that fit your preferences and see if the current volume is high enough to trade.

- Because we only trade five instruments, this is only one of our systems where the position sizing is different—20 percent of your equity per position and maximum five positions.

- Entry Rules
  - Close of the ETF is above the 150-day simple moving average plus one standard deviation (Bollinger band).
  - Enter the next day market on open.

- Exit Rules
  - The close of the ETF is below the 150-day simple moving average minus two standard deviations.
  - Exit the next day market on open.

These ETFs each follow an asset class, so their value will be based on the price of gold or oil, for example. Most of the time, these commodities will not move the same way the broader equities markets move. ETFs, which trade like stocks, are a perfect way to capture trends in noncorrelated markets. I picked these five ETFs because each brings something slightly different to the table. GLD historically does well in times of crisis and inflation. USO is based on crude oil prices, and sometimes those go quite high. DBA is a basket of agricultural commodities like corn, wheat, soybeans, coffee, and cocoa, which are often moved by weather events and trade deals. DBC is a different basket of commodities, such as aluminum and zinc, which move on industrial demand. XLE is the broader energy sector.

Together this is a reasonably diversified portfolio of ETFs that will move differently than the broader market and differently than each other. In comparison to the stock market, these instruments since 2003 have by no means shown the same results—that is *exactly* why you want to trade a basket of these or similar ETFs. The future can be very different; if you add a lot of diversification, that increases the robustness of the suite of systems and the likelihood that when the markets change drastically, you have a better chance to continue to outperform.

The list of ETFs I have included here are suggestions; I encourage you to broaden the list if you want, but remember to seek ETFs that are not going to correlate to the broader market. Also, seek liquidity because you want to be sure the ETF is tradable at all times—be wary of those that have thin trading volumes. Conceptually, you're seeking ETFs that make sense in terms of noncorrelation and inflation hedging.

A Note About Bitcoin

When I built this ETF system, I consciously chose not to include Bitcoin because it has had such an extraordinary performance in recent years (it has risen—unevenly—from about $7,000 to $100,000 from the beginning of 2020 to late 2024 and shown even crazier returns in earlier time periods). The results of including Bitcoin would skew the performance of the system positively, and I'm not confident that such a result can be repeated. Remember, the point of backtesting is to gain insight into likely future performance. I'm not confident, given how new cryptocurrency is and how quickly it has run up, that we should make any inferences from past performance. While the increase in Bitcoin's value in recent years has been extraordinary, I feel that it is now a more mature cryptocurrency and security, and that run-up is not likely to be repeated. In order to be conservative in my projections and not give an inflated projection of future system performance, I have omitted it from these systems. However, I do trade Bitcoin myself, so you can certainly look for a Bitcoin ETF and include it in the portfolio if you believe in the concept.

The objective of this system is to hedge against inflation. During inflationary periods the price of equities generally will rise as the price of everything rises and companies charge more and earn more. Commodities, however, tend to do very well during inflationary periods.

Our investment strategy, embedded in the entry rules, is to look for a long-term upward trend. If such a trend exists, we enter and stay in until the trend expires. We don't have to rank investments because our universe of investments is simply these five ETFs. We divide our equity equally between each of them, and for each one, we enter when there is a strong upward trend. We measure that by watching the 150-day simple moving average plus one standard deviation.

We exit when the ETF moves below the 150-day moving average minus two standard deviations. This is the simplest form of trend following: one entry rule, one exit rule, applied to a small universe of potential investments. Whenever you build systems, you can create all kinds of complexity in your rules, but you don't need to. In fact, you shouldn't, for a couple of reasons. First, that complexity can be a way of over-optimizing your systems to tweak your historical performance. Second, complex rules could mean fewer opportunities to get into the market. By adding too many rules and restrictions, you risk not getting in the trade and missing the complete trend. This system is the purest and simplest form of trend following, and since we do not trade on baskets of hundreds or thousands of stocks, we keep it as simple as possible. Measure when it goes up, enter. When the trend stops, exit. No magic needed here. Keep it simple.

There's no real magic about a 150-day lookback. It could be a different time period; the goal is to identify a trend. All trend indicators do is measure the market to identify when you are supposed to make money with the system. With all systems built this way, it's normal that more than 50 percent of your trades will be losing trades, but that's not a problem because your winning trades will be much bigger than your losers.

Results

- CAGR: 5.1 percent
- Maximum drawdown: 29.5 percent
- MAR: 0.17

Those look like terrible results, don't they? Why in the world would you want to create a system like this?

Because of *when* the system makes money.

Equity Curve for System #3 Inflation Hedge

Yearly Return for System #3 Inflation Hedge

Year	Days	End Total Equity	Total Equty Gain/Loss	# Trades	Annual Gain	Benchmark	Comparison
2003	252	$522,122.25	$22,122.25	1	4.42%	22.32%	-17.89%
2004	252	$561,104.90	$38,982.66	0	7.47%	8.99%	-1.53%
2005	252	$643,975.46	$82,870.56	1	14.77%	3.00%	11.77%
2006	251	$651,682.24	$7,706.78	7	1.20%	13.62%	-12.42%
2007	251	$839,995.37	$188,313.13	10	28.90%	3.53%	25.37%
2008	253	$894,590.99	$54,595.62	7	6.50%	-38.49%	44.99%
2009	252	$980,360.38	$85,769.39	9	9.59%	23.45%	-13.87%
2010	252	$1,128,933.98	$148,573.60	12	15.16%	12.78%	2.37%
2011	252	$1,158,527.15	$29,593.17	8	2.62%	0.00%	2.62%
2012	250	$1,071,206.96	($87,320.19)	16	-7.54%	13.41%	-20.94%
2013	252	$1,099,352.72	$28,145.76	10	2.63%	29.60%	-26.97%
2014	252	$1,065,974.18	($33,378.54)	13	-3.04%	11.39%	-14.43%
2015	252	$1,000,297.57	($65,676.61)	10	-6.16%	-0.73%	-5.43%
2016	252	$1,033,753.75	$33,456.18	13	3.34%	9.54%	-6.19%
2017	251	$1,026,005.28	($7,748.47)	13	-0.75%	19.42%	-20.17%
2018	251	$1,024,745.23	($1,260.05)	13	-0.12%	-6.24%	6.11%
2019	252	$970,830.70	($53,914.53)	18	-5.26%	28.88%	-34.14%
2020	253	$983,614.40	$12,783.70	12	1.32%	16.26%	-14.94%
2021	252	$1,233,396.21	$249,781.81	12	25.39%	26.89%	-1.50%
2022	251	$1.464.110.26	$230,714.05	9	18.71%	-19.44%	38.15%
2023	250	$1,405,848.00	($58,262.26)	13	-3.98%	24.23%	-28.21%
2024	185	$1,470,082.27	$64,234.27	13	4.57%	19.97%	-15.40%

This is a good example of a system that makes money when it is supposed to. Remember, this system has two objectives: don't correlate with System #1 or System #2, and make money during inflation. It does both of those things very well. There was a big jump in 2007–2008, during the Great Recession (outperforming equities by almost 45 percent), and again in

2021 and until mid-2022, when inflation was high and we were in a bear market that drove equities down 20 percent. That year it outperformed by 38 percent, creating a huge alpha.

By the way, be careful not to draw the wrong conclusion about 2022. Yes, there was a bear market that year, but this is not a system designed to make money in bear markets. It's a system designed to diversify by asset classes and to make money during inflationary periods, and the inflation rate was 8.0 percent in 2022. That's what mattered for this system. Now, one reason the system works is because people look for other investments during bear markets, creating demand that drives up the prices of commodities. You do have a good chance of doing well with this system during a bear market, but consider that frosting on the cake.

On the other hand, it loses money pretty consistently from 2012 to 2019 because this was a period of very low inflation. For many systematic traders, this is the reason *not* to include a system, but they are dead wrong. This is the crucial part to add to your suite because it has a return stream that is completely different from the previous systems, so it complements them. Also, during this money-losing time, your other systems are making money. The period from 2012 to 2019 was effectively a deflationary period, and I don't care that some of my money was locked up then because this system's investments nearly doubled in value when inflation hit.

Think back to what was happening then. The US government passed massive spending bills to push money into the economy and prevent a consumer spending collapse, which created upward inflationary pressure. Russia invaded

Ukraine, cutting off its grain exports and driving grain prices up. Gold and other commodities (remember copper and lithium?) went up too.

You can see with this system that **what matters is not only the CAGR and the drawdowns but also when a system makes money.** Yes, the CAGR over twenty years is not impressive. But if you ran this system during 2008 and 2022, you'd be very glad you did.

Now let's look at the effect of adding the Inflation Hedge to our first two systems.

Results of Combining Systems #1, #2, and #3

	S&P 500 Trend Following	NASDAQ 100 Trend Following	Inflation Hedge	Combined 33,3% each
CAGR	19.9%	23.8%	5.1%	**18.2%**
Max Drawdown	32.9%	41.3%	29.5%	**22.6%**
MAR	0.61	0.58	0.17	**0.80**

Let's compare this to the S&P 500.

	S&P 500	Combined Suite of Three Systems	Difference
CAGR	8.8%	18.2%	**9.4% more CAGR**
Max Drawdown	56.7%	22.6%	**34.1% less drawdown**
MAR	0.16	0.80	**0.64 higher MAR**

CAGR drops 4.7 percent from the combination of Systems #1 and #2, but the maximum drawdown falls 9.9 percent, and MAR rises to 0.80. So while we've trimmed our overall return, we've really reduced our drawdowns, and that's where an investor feels the pain. Lowering that drawdown makes a big difference for your peace of mind.

Equity Curve for Systems 1, 2, and 3 Combined

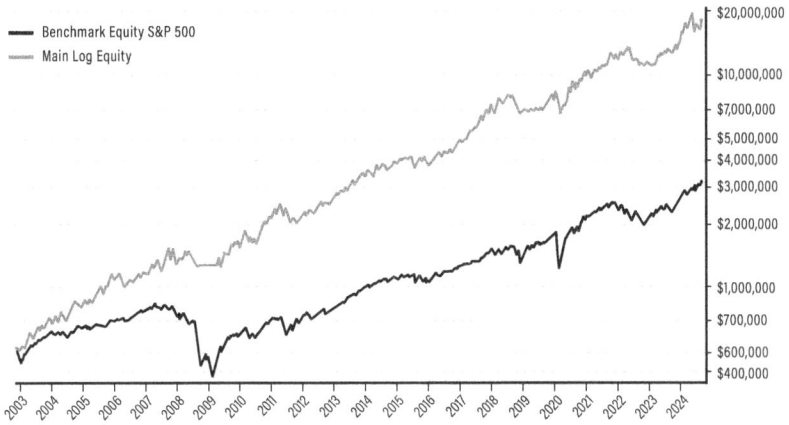

Legend:
- Benchmark Equity S&P 500
- Main Log Equity

Yearly Results for Systems #1, #2, and #3 Combined

Combined, the systems still lose money in 2008, 2011, and 2022 (see the table on the next page). But the losses are much less than the broader equity market experienced. You can see from the equity curve that there was a point in 2008 when all the systems went to cash. Yes, we were in an overall drawdown, but it was much less than the total market drawdown. Plenty of investors would have been delighted to go through the Great Recession with only a 17 percent drawdown in their portfolios.

This is incredibly important for capital preservation. If you experience a drawdown of 50 percent, you have to get a 100 percent return just to get back to where you started. With a 16.45 percent drawdown, as the combined systems

Year	Days	End Total Equity	Total Equty	# Trades	Annual Gain
2003	252	$692,043.72	$192,043.72	55	38.41%
2004	252	$868,293.15	$176,249.43	60	25.47%
2005	252	$1,084,319.74	$216,026.59	89	24.88%
2006	251	$1,161,344.37	$77,024.63	81	7.10%
2007	251	$1,527,704.14	$366,359.77	104	31.55%
2008	253	$1.276,323.08	($251,381.06)	65	-16.45%
2009	252	$1,656,669.54	$380,346.46	93	29.80%
2010	252	$2,087,928.96	$431,259.42	84	26.03%
2011	252	$2,067,667.99	($20,260.98)	84	-0.97%
2012	250	$2,471,148.41	$403,480.42	73	19.51%
2013	252	$3,494,552.68	$1,023,404.27	39	41.41%
2014	252	$3,947,110.33	$452,557.65	61	12.95%
2015	252	$4,141,036.02	$193,925.69	72	4.91%
2016	252	$4,666,252.63	$525,216.61	91	12.68%
2017	251	$6,565,204.90	$1,898,952.27	35	40.70%
2018	251	$6,709,892.79	$144,687.89	76	2.20%
2019	252	$7,736,602.97	$1,026,710.19	77	15.30%
2020	253	$10,021,223.03	$2,284,620.06	64	29.53%
2021	252	$12,807,491.59	$2,786,268.56	62	27.80%
2022	251	$11,332,552.33	($1,474,939.27)	101	-11.52%
2023	250	$13,720,017.43	$2,387,465.10	87	21.07%
2024	185	$18,903,408.04	$5,183,390.62	53	37.78%

experienced in 2008, you will be back to your starting point once you earn 20 percent. That is much, much easier to do and gets you back to growing your assets and compounding your returns sooner. An approach like this could save your retirement.

But is it enough? Let's add another loosely correlated system.

CHAPTER 7

SYSTEM #4: TREND FOLLOWING ON ENERGY STOCKS

As WE CONTINUE TO SMOOTH THE EQUITY CURVE, WE'RE GOING to add in another trend following system, this one focused on energy. This is just one example of a sector where we can find stocks that at times can be very noncorrelated to the broader market. There are many opportunities to create systems that focus on specific sectors; I trade fifty-five different systems in my own portfolio, many of them like this. Look at this example as a framework for what you can build.

Objective

In System #1 and System #2, we focused on the broader market, with relatively long lookbacks for the trend rules, of 200 and 100 days respectively. System #3 was created with simple trend rules with a 150-day lookback on a portfolio with very diversified assets traded through ETFs.

In this new system we aim, through sector diversification, to trade a portfolio that possibly contains stocks that act very differently than the broader market. I choose in this case to only trade energy stocks. Also, we want to have a faster entry on the trend, and exit. A third rule, to make sure there is zero overlap with the other systems, is to make sure that we diversify by liquidity. The first two equity systems all focused on big indices and very liquid stocks, while this system will look at other stocks.

So how can we achieve these three objectives?

Rules

- Sector diversification
  - Trading universe: All energy stocks.

- Liquidity filter
  - Minimum price: one US dollar.
  - Average minimum volume of 500,000 shares over the last fifty days.

- Entry rules
  - Faster lookback of the trend
    - The close of the S&P 1500 energy sector is above the 50-day exponential moving average.
    - The close of the stock is above the 50-day Keltner channel plus 2 ATR for the last twenty-one days.
  - Ranking: If we have more candidates than we are allowed to trade (ten positions maximum), priority goes to the stocks with the lowest average dollar volume over the last fifty days (but still liquid enough, as you see in the filters).
  - Buy the next day on a stop order 0.5 ATR above today's close.

- Exit rules
  - Stop loss of 1 ATR.
  - Trailing stop of 20 percent.
  - If either is triggered, exit the next day at market price on open.

We want to make sure that we don't bet too heavily on the S&P 500 and the NASDAQ 100. With this system, we're working in a distinct asset class. While energy stocks can correlate with the broader economy—for example, they dropped in March 2020 when COVID shut down the economy. But when the market is flatter, they can do well.

As with our other trend following systems, our first rule looks for an upward trend in the sector we're working in—the S&P 1500 energy sector. Our lookback is different from the System #1 (two hundred days) and System #2 (one hundred days). Here we look back fifty days, which gives us differentiation.

We find an edge with this system with ranking. Priority goes to stocks with the lowest average dollar volume. That means we'll be able to invest in stocks that the big institutions are not invested in. If you look for stocks with the lowest volume, you are almost certain not to be in a stock that is also in the S&P 500 or the NASDAQ 100. We have to be careful to seek liquidity, though, so we also have rules for minimum price and minimum dollar volume.

The last entry rule—buy on a stop order 0.5 ATR above today's close—ensures that the stock has intraday upward momentum.

Results

- CAGR: 14.3 percent
- Maximum drawdown: 52 percent

That looks pretty terrible, doesn't it? Your first instinct might be to try to optimize the system to reduce the drawdown. That's the wrong response. I put this system in because I want you to understand that individual systems will experience drawdowns of 50 percent or even more, yet they still can be important to you portfolio.

What matters more than the drawdown is when this system makes money.

Equity Curve for System #4 Energy Stocks

Yearly Results for System #4

Look at 2008 and 2022! The delta against the S&P 500 was almost 60 percent and 93 percent, respectively. This system

Year	Days	End Total Equity	Total Equty Gain/Loss	# Trades	Annual Gain	Benchmark	Comparison
2003	252	$699,859.62	$199,859.62	94	39.97%	22.32%	17.65%
2004	252	$948,590.99	$248,731.37	50	35.54%	8.99%	26.55%
2005	252	$1,331,457.67	$382,866.68	47	40.36%	3.00%	37.36%
2006	251	$1,535,216.30	$203,758.63	90	15.30%	13.62%	1.68%
2007	251	$1,879,338.78	$344,122.48	65	22.42%	3.53%	18.89%
2008	253	$2,200.861.77	$321,522.99	60	17.11%	-38.49%	55.59%
2009	252	$2,832,490.25	$631,628.48	114	28.70%	23.45%	5.24%
2010	252	$4,609,486.73	$1,776,996.48	62	62.74%	12.78%	49.95%
2011	252	$4,354,391.44	($255,095.29)	109	-5.53%	0.00%	-5.53%
2012	250	$3,758,247.78	($596,143.66)	106	-13.69%	13.41%	-27.10%
2013	252	$4,619,747.51	$861,499.74	65	22.92%	29.60%	-6.68%
2014	252	$4,185,983.77	($433,763.74)	78	-9.39%	11.39%	-20.78%
2015	252	$3,344,777.43	($841,206.34)	96	-20.10%	-0.73%	-19.37%
2016	252	$5,881,234.00	$2,536,456.56	89	75.83%	9.54%	66.30%
2017	251	$5,882,153.26	$919.26	71	0.02%	19.42%	-19.40%
2018	251	$4,934,948.00	($947,205.26)	66	-16.10%	-6.24%	-9.87%
2019	252	$5,589,306.92	$654,358.93	95	13.26%	28.88%	-15.62%
2020	253	$3,897,584.04	($1,691,722.88)	115	-30.27%	16.26%	-46.53%
2021	252	$5,181,713.06	$1,284,129.02	70	32.95%	26.89%	6.05%
2022	251	$8,993,797.50	$3,812,084.44	76	73.57%	-19.44%	93.01%
2023	250	$10,468,522.11	$1,474,724.61	81	16.40%	24.23%	-7.83%
2024	185	$9,147,902.58	($1,320,619.53)	88	-12.62%	19.97%	-32.58%

makes money when it really needs to make money, and it experiences drawdowns during periods when other systems will make them up. I get more excited when I see a system like this than one that's a steady earner because I know how powerful it will be in combination with other systems.

Now that we have four systems, let's look at the equity curve of each on the same chart.

Equity Curve for Systems #1, #2, #3, and #4

Here's where we can actually see the noncorrelation. For example, Inflation Hedge does great in 2008 when the S&P and NASDAQ are falling. Energy jumps in 2017 when the other three are flat or falling. Both Energy and Inflation Hedge have big gains in 2022 when the NASDAQ and S&P aren't doing well.

You can see the relative correlations of the four systems numerically here. This is a table that shows the daily percentile correlation of each system.

Four Systems Correlation Matrix

Following System	S&P 500 Trend	NASDAQ 100 Trend	Inflation Hedge ETF	Energy Trend
S&P500 Trend	100	72	25	37
Nasdaq 100	72	100	15	25
Inflation Hedge ETF	25	15	100	51
Energy Trend	37	25	51	100

Not surprisingly, the S&P 500 and NASDAQ 100 systems correlate closely with each other (0 means no correlation at all; 100 means perfect correlation). But the Inflation Hedge has a correlation index of 15 with the NASDAQ 100, and the Energy system has a correlation index of 37 with the S&P 500.

Let's look at how our suite of systems performs when we devote 25 percent of our equity to each system.

Combined Results of Trend Following Systems 1, 2, 3, and 4

	Trend following systems 1, 2, 3, and 4	S&P 500	Compared to benchmark
CAGR	18.01%	8.8%	**9.2% more CAGR**
Maximum drawdown	23.7%	56.7%	**33% less drawdown**
Longest drawdown	29 months	65 months	**36 fewer months**
MAR	0.76	0.16	**0.6 better MAR**

If you remember the combined results from the first three systems (shown in the previous chapter), you'll see that these are slightly worse. The CAGR drops 0.1 percent, and the maximum drawdown increases 1.5 percent. Why would you want to include the Energy system given those results?

For an answer, let's look at the annual returns.

Yearly Results for Combined Systems #1, #2, #3, and #4

Until we added System #4, we were losing money in 2022. Now we are making money that year, and we've cut the 2008 drawdown from more than 16 percent to 8.49 percent. We outperform the broader market by 30 percent in 2008

Year	Days	End Total Equity	Total Equty Gain/Loss	# Trades	Annual Gain	Benchmark	Comparison
2003	252	$695,249.54	$195,249.54	149	39.05%	22.32%	16.73%
2004	252	$886,303.47	$191,053.93	110	27.48%	8.99%	18.49%
2005	252	$1,144,381.57	$258,078.11	136	29.12%	3.00%	26.12%
2006	251	$1,256,390.57	$112,009.00	171	9.79%	13.62%	-3.83%
2007	251	$1,621,175.14	$364,784.57	169	29.03%	3.53%	25.50%
2008	253	$1,483,553.74	($137,621.40)	125	-8.49%	-38.49%	30.00%
2009	252	$1,932,404.41	$448,850.67	207	30.26%	23.45%	6.80%
2010	252	$2,604,735.61	$672,331.20	146	34.79%	12.78%	22.01%
2011	252	$2,551,548.81	($53,186.80)	193	-2.04%	0.00%	-2.04%
2012	250	$2,835,671.70	$284,122.88	179	11.14%	13.41%	-2.27%
2013	252	$3,931,297.93	$1,095,626.24	104	38.64%	29.60%	9.04%
2014	252	$4,247,145.31	$315,847.38	139	8.03%	11.39%	-3.36%
2015	252	$4,206,320.14	($40,825.17)	168	-0.96%	-0.73%	-0.23%
2016	252	$5,255,546.51	$1,049,226.36	180	24.94%	9.54%	15.41%
2017	251	$6,839,615.38	$1,584,068.88	106	30.14%	19.42%	10.72%
2018	251	$6,626,721.45	($212,893.93)	142	-3.11%	-6.24%	3.12%
2019	252	$7,613,677.67	$986,956.21	172	14.89%	28.88%	-13.98%
2020	253	$8,640,315.12	$1,026,637.46	179	13.48%	16.26%	-2.77%
2021	252	$11,265,963.68	$2,625,648.56	132	30.39%	26.89%	3.50%
2022	251	$11,986,060.55	$720,096.87	177	6.39%	-19.44%	25.83%
2023	250	$14,461,655.14	$2,475,594.59	168	20.65%	24.23%	-3.58%
2024	185	$18,075,057.48	$3,613,402.34	141	24.99%	19.97%	5.02%

and almost 26 percent in 2022. The equity curve is looking smoother. More importantly, we also add another layer of diversification by building a system in a different sector and with a different entry and exit frequency. This increases the likelihood of creating a more robust suite of systems.

Equity Curve for Combined Systems #1, #2, #3, and #4

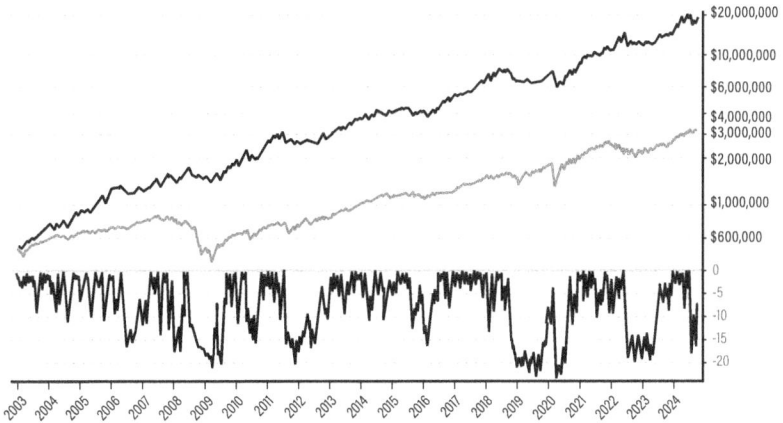

Recap of the Trend Following Systems

We now have four systems, all of them in the trend following style. They look for upward trends in whatever market universe they are paying attention to and in individual stocks. Each has a different universe and different entry rules, which diversifies by the frequency (50 days, 100 days, 150 days, and 200 days), which combine to reduce the correlation between the systems.

System #1 trades in the S&P 500 and looks for the most liquid stocks. It has a two-hundred-day lookback for both the market and individual stocks and gives preference to the stocks with the highest relative strength.

System #2 trades in the NASDAQ 100 and has a one-hundred-day lookback for the market and individual stocks. Both have to be trending up, and it looks for the stocks with high volume.

79

System #3 trades sector-focused ETFs that specialize in different commodities that do not generally correlate with equities markets. It has a 150-day lookback.

System #4 trades energy stocks, filtering for those with the lowest average dollar volume. This means the system focuses on stocks not traded by big institutions. The lookback is only fifty days long for both the sector and individual stocks.

All these systems are designed to get into trades on upward momentum and ride them until there is a strongly established downturn. They give away a significant chunk of profit, but the winning trades do very well.

So far, so good. But all these systems rely on a rising market or at least market sector. As we know, the market doesn't always rise. Importantly, with trend following systems, we can only trade long. Because of the rules around trading retirement accounts, it's difficult or impossible to trade short. So what else can we do?

Let's look at our second investing approach, mean reversion, to build our remaining systems, reduce correlation, and improve results.

CHAPTER 8

SYSTEM #5: "CATCH A FALLING KNIFE IN AN UPTREND" MEAN REVERSION

I RECOMMEND COMMITTING 50 PERCENT OF YOUR ASSETS TO your trend following systems and 50 percent to mean reversion long. But depending on your preference, this allocation could be different for you. Some people prefer trend following systems, and others prefer shorter-term systems like those I am about to describe. Both have pros and cons.

But why do we want to include mean reversion at all? Those four LTTF systems perform well, don't they? Yes, they test well from 2003. But there are periods where they don't do as well, particularly in sideways markets. And because we are buying fear when we trade mean reversion long, we'll see a lot of noncorrelation compared to the trend following systems (which buy greed).

While LTTF systems tend to have long-duration trades for those positions that are performing well, mean reversion trades are short, generally lasting two to five days. Consequently, a long-term trend following system is likely to execute very few trades a year, while a mean reversion system may have two hundred or three hundred trades. Rather than trying to make a lot of money over a long period of time on a single trade, MR systems aim to make a little money over and over again, which can add up to a nice compound annual return. Mean reversion can complement LTTF systems, particularly in sideways markets where there are not clear upward trends. They generally underperform LTTF systems in a bull market, but that's fine.

Let's look at our first system, which is designed to get into a stock right at the bottom of a temporary dip.

Objective

We want to take advantage of the fact that we are able to trade in a universe of stocks that most institutional investors are not allowed to (because the price or volume is below their required minimums), which gives us an extra edge if we buy these stocks while they are up-trending and have a sell-off. We buy them when they are oversold, taking advantage of the panic and know that our statistical likelihood that they revert to the mean is more than 50 percent.

Rules

- Trading universe: All US stocks, excluding OTC stocks

- Filters
  - Minimum price: five US dollars.
  - Daily volume: minimum 500,000 daily average over the last 50 days.
  - Historic volatility: At least 30.

- Setups
  - Close of the stock is above the 252-day (one calendar year in trading days) SMA.
  - Today was a down day, and the relative strength index (RSI) is below 15.

- Ranking: If we have more candidates that we can trade, we give preference to the stocks with the highest twenty-day historic volatility.

- Entry
  - Maximum of ten orders.
  - Tomorrow, we place a maximum of ten limit orders, 0.75 ATR (ten-day lookback) below today's close.

- Exits:
  - Stop loss: If the close is 2 ATR (10) lower than our entry price.
  - We place a profit target tomorrow of 4 percent above the execution price, and if this price is hit during the day, we sell.
  - We have a time-based exit of four days. If we have not already, we exit the next day on the close.

This system is designed to catch a falling knife in an uptrend. In other words, we're looking for individual stocks that are on an upward trend but have been oversold; we want to get in just before they recover. There is a higher-than-average statistical likelihood that the oversold stock will revert to its upward trend; that reversion back toward its mean is the delta that we want to capture.

We exclude OTC stocks from the trading universe; I tend to avoid them in general because you don't know what you're getting.

Because the market has a long bias, a long lookback ensures we find more stocks we could trade, and high trade frequency is important for the system. For that same reason, we seek stocks with higher volatility (30 or more) because we want stocks that are moving a lot. (For comparison, the S&P 500 has an average historic volatility of about 19.)

We're looking for stocks that show a long upward trend (they are above their 252-day SMA) and are oversold; the "RSI below 15" rule is the indicator of a stock being oversold. That tells us we have an opportunity to buy a rising stock on the cheap. We buy on a day limit order—not a "good 'til canceled" (GTC) order—of 0.75 ATR below today's close because we want to get into stocks that are being pummeled. We're looking for the stock to go even lower than it is before buying. You can place up to ten limit orders (we don't take more than ten positions in the system), but don't expect them all to be filled. If a stock has fallen 1 ATR over the previous ten days of 10 percent, we're looking for it to drop another 7.5 percent (0.75 ATR) before we enter, and not every candidate will do that. A stock may only decline another 0.5 ATR before rebounding, or it may revert immediately on open. If that happens, your limit order won't be filled.

It's reasonable to expect this system to be fully invested only 20 percent of the time on average. Sometimes you won't be invested at all because there are no candidates or because the candidates you identify don't meet the requirements of your entry orders. There will be times, though, when the whole market is still in a long-term uptrend and sells off on a short-term basis, and this system is fully exposed.

Now let's look at the exit rules. We have to give this system room to breathe—this is the "catch a falling knife" part. Our intent is to get into a stock right at the bottom, before it reverts. But we might get in while it's still on the way down. It's going to revert eventually, but it hasn't hit bottom yet. We set a stop loss of 2 ATR to give it room to descend further before recovering. Of course, it might not recover, so if it keeps going down, we'll be stopped out.

We have a profit target of 4 percent from the entry point; we hit that, we're out. As I mentioned above, the strategy behind this system is to compound many small, profitable trades. Finally, there's a time-based exit; if we haven't made money in the last four days, we get out. We don't want to leave capital tied up in stocks that aren't performing because this system demands a high trade frequency to generate a return.

Results for System #5

- CAGR: 16.6 percent
- Maximum drawdown: 21.1 percent
- Longest drawdown: 20.3 months
- MAR: 0.78
- Winning trade percentage: 67 percent

Our four previous systems had a combined longest drawdown of 29.6 months; this system has a substantially shorter drawdown of 20.3 months. Why? Because of trade frequency. System #5 looks for candidates in a universe of approximately seven thousand listed stocks, and it finds profitable opportunities for mean reversion sooner and more frequently than our LTTF systems, which look at smaller trading universes.

Equity Curve for System #5 "Catch a Falling Knife" Mean Reversion

When you look at the equity curve above, I bet the first thing you notice is that this system made money in 2008. Don't be misled! That was a happy coincidence because the system is not designed to make money in bear markets. It certainly can happen as there are pullbacks and some up-trending stocks, but that result did not happen on purpose. I happened to trade a similar system in 2008 live, and I did make a lot of money trading MR long as that was a bear market with a lot of pullbacks. There is *no* guarantee.

A more likely outcome is what happened in August 2011, when the system dropped 11.28 percent in a single month, correlating with the benchmark index, which fell about 17 percent. This behavior makes sense when you think about how the system functions. You are looking to buy stocks that are generally on the rise but have been sold off. Because the market declined so rapidly, our lookback in early August shows that the stock is on a rise and appears to be in a brief decline, so we buy. But the whole market is declining, and our positions keep falling, which leads to being stopped out with a loss. This performance is something you should expect with a mean reversion system that has a long lookback filter.

Also, at this time, I was trading a few more mean reversion systems, and it was the first time I had a drawdown that was larger than my backtest. I was stunned, in total disbelief. But if you look at it objectively, and the market sells off in lockstep, it is totally understandable that something like that would happen.

You can get caught in a period where individual stocks fit your purchase rules but the market as a whole is dropping and they don't revert to their mean. (We see another example of this in March 2022.) Your system will lose money if the market as a whole moves against you. Similarly, when the market is very bullish, such as in 2023 and 2024, the system also will underperform because there will not be as many opportunities.

Let's look at where the system does make money—2004–2007 is a good example. We see on the equity curve the widening delta between the benchmark performance and the system performance, kicked off by very good results in 2004, when the market largely went sideways. That's a great market for a system like this one.

One final thing to notice on the equity curve is the recovery from the sharp drawdowns in 2011 and 2022. The system hits its maximum drawdown but almost immediately recovers 5 or 10 percent because some of the positions turn around at the bottom. In those cases, the system is working again; we make a quick profit and get out. That recovers some of the initial loss.

Monthly and Annual Returns for System #5

This system likes volatility. It did very well in 2021. But when the entire market turns down, as it did in August 2011 or during the COVID sell-off, this system becomes very correlated with your LTTF systems. In that situation, your mean reversion orders are getting filled but then stopping out with a loss at the same time that your LTTF systems are stopping out with losses. This is clearly a problem. We can address it with a mean reversion system that is unlikely to be in the market when it takes a broad downturn.

Year	Jan	Feb	Mar	Apr	May	Jun	Jul	Aug	Sep	Oct	Nov	Dec	Annual Gain	Benchmark	Comparison
2003	2.50%	1.08%	1.39%	0.41%	1.82%	0.77%	3.82%	3.44%	-2.66%	5.70%	2.28%	4.97%	28.39%	22.32%	6.07%
2004	3.75%	8.97%	4.48%	-0.30%	10.01%	1.30%	-1.08%	0.47%	0.91%	2.00%	-1.61%	6.87%	41.15%	8.99%	32.16%
2005	-1.55%	2.30%	2.19%	-0.61%	2.75%	1.60%	0.95%	4.17%	0.33%	2.63%	2.36%	1.31%	19.91%	3.00%	16.91%
2006	2.15%	2.68%	0.08%	1.27%	3.46%	-0.79%	-0.46%	2.77%	-1.14%	1.13%	1.91%	1.68%	15.64%	13.62%	2.02%
2007	2.08%	-1.80%	0.20%	0.42%	3.70%	0.63%	-1.54%	10.77%	1.11%	2.04%	1.19%	0.33%	20.33%	3.53%	16.80%
2008	-1.59%	-0.55%	-4.06%	-0.46%	0.50%	0.27%	7.82%	2.09%	-1.31%	9.06%	0.37%	1.21%	13.36%	-38.49%	51.85%
2009	0.60%	-0.15%	-0.40%	0.38%	1.85%	1.28%	2.72%	1.86%	-0.56%	-4.83%	0.72%	4.80%	8.28%	23.45%	-15.17%
2010	1.44%	6.15%	0.84%	1.33%	4.75%	0.84%	1.70%	0.31%	0.82%	0.94%	1.02%	3.13%	25.70%	12.78%	12.92%
2011	3.82%	1.14%	4.93%	4.64%	2.99%	1.86%	1.02%	-11.28%	-0.63%	3.28%	0.06%	0.06%	11.39%	0.00%	11.39%
2012	0.76%	0.54%	2.64%	-3.63%	-4.43%	1.06%	1.47%	1.39%	-0.36%	1.28%	2.34%	0.80%	3.64%	13.41%	-9.76%
2013	0.97%	0.78%	2.61%	6.03%	4.08%	3.26%	1.70%	0.87%	2.24%	1.29%	0.26%	1.07%	28.08%	29.60%	-1.53%
2014	-0.47%	3.94%	-0.68%	3.36%	0.82%	-0.64%	1.54%	0.60%	1.34%	-2.95%	0.23%	0.03%	7.16%	11.39%	-4.23%
2015	3.25%	1.39%	2.12%	-3.63%	7.10%	4.47%	5.79%	2.81%	-6.81%	4.96%	-0.19%	-1.66%	20.38%	-0.73%	21.11%
2016	-5.58%	1.91%	-0.57%	0.80%	0.73%	1.41%	0.49%	-2.26%	4.55%	-3.98%	1.44%	0.46%	-1.02%	9.54%	-10.55%
2017	1.52%	-2.97%	5.71%	0.55%	1.91%	4.18%	0.03%	-2.39%	1.38%	-0.64%	1.76%	2.89%	14.48%	19.42%	-4.94%
2018	2.17%	2.64%	5.98%	-0.40%	0.14%	5.83%	2.42%	1.99%	4.77%	-7.04%	0.61%	-1.09%	18.76%	-6.24%	25.00%
2019	0.00%	0.58%	-1.06%	1.19%	-0.12%	0.23%	2.21%	-3.15%	1.72%	2.90%	1.14%	2.63%	8.42%	28.88%	-20.46%
2020	0.38%	-3.10%	-11.36%	0.00%	3.01%	0.96%	3.73%	6.10%	6.23%	-1.28%	7.32%	3.93%	15.43%	16.26%	-0.83%
2021	8.86%	7.66%	5.83%	2.38%	3.70%	-1.63%	9.19%	1.66%	2.18%	3.07%	0.64%	9.53%	66.92%	26.89%	40.03%
2022	1.00%	0.57%	1.23%	-8.41%	-0.73%	-5.40%	1.64%	0.40%	-1.52%	0.62%	3.35%	-3.36%	-10.67%	-19.44%	8.78%
2023	0.75%	-1.75%	18.53%	-2.61%	-1.82%	0.50%	0.83%	0.18%	0.19%	1.76%	1.54%	0.81%	18.85%	24.23%	-5.38%
2024	1.71%	0.40%	-0.39%	-3.81%	0.82%	0.12%	3.06%	-0.16%	2.96%	0.00%	0.00%	0.00%	4.63%	19.97%	-15.33%

CHAPTER 9

SYSTEM #6: SHORT LOOKBACK MEAN REVERSION

IF YOU'RE NOT IN THE MARKET WHEN IT STARTS TO FALL, YOU won't lose money. How do we accomplish that? With a simple filter that prohibits us from placing entry orders at the first sign of market decline. We do that with a shorter lookback filter.

Objective

Buy upward trending stocks on a pullback and limit the potential downside, preserving capital. This means two things:

- Only buy when the market as a whole is in an uptrend, and make sure that if there is even the slightest sign of a possible extended sell-off, do not place new orders.

- Have a very short time duration so that if the market sell-off continues you are not dragged down for four or five days, and instead limit the pain and get out after one day.

The whole objective is to not be in the market when carnage happens. This lowers the combined drawdowns because all other systems are losing during that time.

Rules

- Trading universe: All US stocks, excluding OTC stocks.

- Filters
  - Minimum price: one US dollar.
  - Daily volume: average 500,000 daily over the last fifty days.
  - Minimum ATR percentage is more than 5 (this is the ATR expressed as a percentage of the closing price).

- Setups
  - Close of the S&P 500 index (SPY) is above the 40-day exponential moving average.
  - Close of the stock is above the 40-day exponential moving average.
  - Seven-day ADX is above 30.
  - Three-day RSI of the stock is below 25.
  - Rank stocks by the lowest three-day RSI.

- Entry
  - Place a limit order the next day of 0.7 ATR (over the last ten days) below the previous close.

- Exit

  - Exit next day, market on close.

S&P Exponential Moving Average During Covid Crash

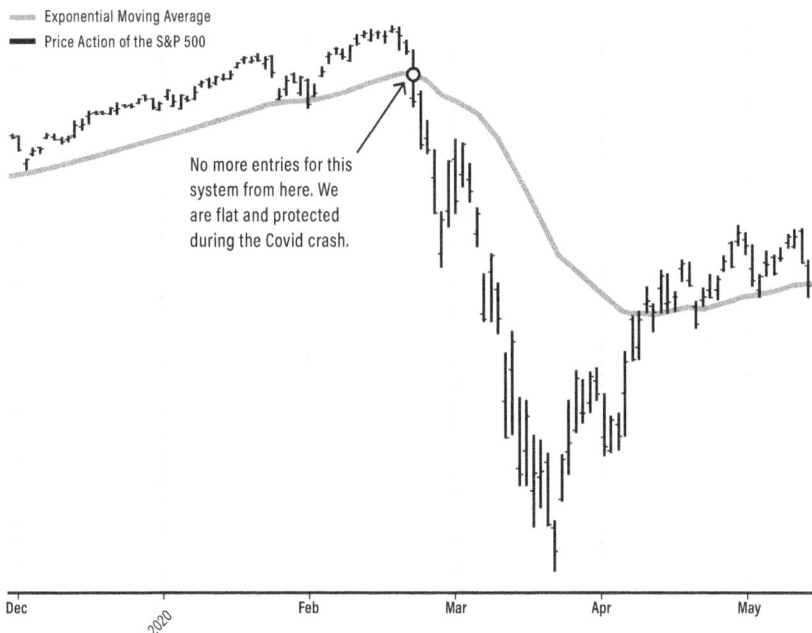

Exponential Moving Average
Price Action of the S&P 500

No more entries for this system from here. We are flat and protected during the Covid crash.

Dec   2020   Feb   Mar   Apr   May

As soon as the S&P 500 closed below the forty-day exponential moving average, the system went to cash, which means it remained flat throughout that big and painful drop.

The filters give us liquidity, via daily volume, and volatility. A minimum ten-day ATR of more than 5 percent indicates a relatively volatile stock.

The first rule in the setup is key. We are only going to trade if the market is trading above the forty-day exponential moving average, which gives more weight to recent market price action. It will respond fairly quickly if the market begins to fall. If the stock is above the forty-day exponential moving average, it's been doing well. It also is a protective rule because when the market drops below the forty-day EMA, we are flat.

The ADX is a neutral trend measurement—it measures movement but does not measure whether it's rising or falling. We want a stock that is moving, so the ADX has to be above 30.

Finally, we're looking for stocks with a three-day RSI below 25, and we rank them with the lowest three-day RSI first. That puts us in stocks that are oversold.

We get in with a limit order of 0.7 ATR (ten-day) below the previous close. As with System #5, we're looking for stocks that are pummeled. Finally, you'll see what might seem like a surprising exit rule: we get out the following day on close, regardless of the stock's performance. This is the other part of getting out of bear markets quickly. There is a statistically greater than average chance that we have gotten into a stock that is going to begin to revert toward the mean the next day, which will yield a profit. But if we've gotten in at the beginning of a more severe drop, we don't want to stay in. If we had an exit rule of, say, "exit after five days on close" if the stock has not turned a profit, we could suffer severe losses. To prevent this, we dip our toe in, look to make a quick profit, and jump back out, profit or no. Our preference with this system is to be out of the market at the whiff of a downturn.

This system is very focused on limiting potential downside while making money where it can. The whole objective of this system is to blunt the drawdowns that happen to our first mean reversion system (System #5) in sharp market selloffs like August 2011 and March 2020. We make money because the rules ensure that we do have a statistical edge to find the upside in stocks, and it does a good job of not losing money.

Results

- CAGR: 17.08 percent
- Maximum drawdown: 25.63 percent
- Longest drawdown: 32 months
- MAR: 0.67
- Winning trades percentage: 57 percent

Looking at these results, you might wonder why it has such a substantial drawdown since the system is built to avoid being caught in a bear market. This can be explained by the exit rule. The system will identify stocks that are indeed going to revert to their mean, but they don't do so quickly enough for the system to capture that profit (remember, they have to at least begin to revert the next trading day to capture the profit). If this failure to revert quickly happens enough, the system will be in drawdown.

Equity Curve of System #6 Short Lookback Mean Reversion

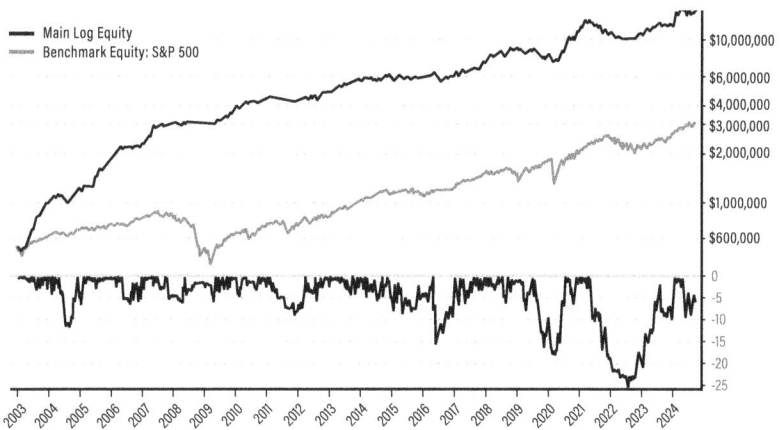

95

Let's look at what happened in August 2011 and March 2020, the two months that have been plaguing our performance so far. All long systems that were in the market in August 2011 and during the COVID sell-off in March 2020 lost significant money. **This system, per design, was flat during these big market selloffs**, which lowers the combined drawdown.

Monthly and Annual Returns for System #6

In both of those months, this system returned exactly zero, and that's exactly what we want to have happen.

Look at what happens in the months following March 2020: the system jumps in as the market recovers and starts to quickly generate returns. It makes significant profits very quickly. This is another benefit of a short lookback. We are looking for upward trend signals on the forty-day exponential moving average. We'll see them much sooner than we will in systems that have longer lookbacks.

Where did the system notably lose money? The biggest drop was in September 2021, down 9 percent, but that came at a time when the other systems we trade were doing well. That's exactly what we want as we work to smooth the equity curve.

When we combine the two mean reversion systems, trading 50 percent of our equity with each, this is what happens.

Year	Jan	Feb	Mar	Apr	May	Jun	Jul	Aug	Sep	Oct	Nov	Dec	Annual Gain
2003	3.02%	0.00%	2.15%	6.82%	8.69%	12.89%	13.15%	4.53%	3.20%	12.37%	3.52%	0.88%	97.58%
2004	3.14%	7.81%	2.63%	-2.92%	-0.10%	-7.04%	-0.62%	0.67%	1.65%	4.73%	8.60%	3.64%	23.33%
2005	-1.68%	5.45%	0.96%	-0.07%	-1.02%	13.05%	6.08%	5.16%	1.56%	1.04%	3.85%	6.86%	48.72%
2006	7.06%	0.60%	8.36%	4.70%	-2.13%	0.00%	-1.02%	2.17%	1.76%	-1.69%	1.89%	2.61%	26.50%
2007	3.87%	8.66%	0.72%	11.57%	2.54%	1.96%	-2.11%	0.00%	3.89%	3.77%	-4.89%	0.54%	33.84%
2008	0.00%	-1.22%	0.00%	2.32%	1.16%	-0.67%	0.00%	1.05%	0.72%	0.00%	0.00%	-0.18%	3.18%
2009	0.06%	-0.50%	-2.14%	1.42%	3.08%	0.45%	3.48%	-0.22%	2.11%	3.59%	4.11%	4.60%	21.68%
2010	-1.12%	1.53%	3.28%	3.59%	-0.57%	0.00%	0.06%	-1.69%	1.40%	5.10%	3.38%	1.30%	17.25%
2011	-0.75%	-1.06%	0.90%	-0.33%	-2.24%	-0.04%	-2.31%	0.00%	-0.26%	0.08%	-1.00%	-0.38%	-7.19%
2012	2.03%	-0.75%	5.79%	0.73%	-1.95%	-0.32%	-1.32%	2.77%	4.24%	1.48%	0.00%	-1.58%	11.37%
2013	1.51%	3.36%	1.91%	4.29%	2.21%	1.32%	0.46%	-1.36%	3.12%	0.04%	1.83%	-0.04%	20.19%
2014	3.20%	1.53%	0.71%	-0.95%	-2.10%	-0.44%	0.26%	1.22%	1.86%	1.21%	2.00%	-2.47%	6.02%
2015	-2.39%	2.62%	2.29%	-3.24%	-0.02%	-0.70%	1.69%	-2.45%	0.00%	1.50%	1.10%	0.58%	0.78%
2016	0.28%	-1.28%	2.48%	5.53%	-6.42%	-7.17%	1.43%	0.76%	2.71%	0.03%	1.87%	3.27%	2.73%
2017	-1.32%	7.32%	2.44%	-4.17%	-0.12%	1.26%	4.06%	0.64%	2.66%	2.24%	2.05%	7.24%	26.47%
2018	3.88%	2.10%	-2.13%	-0.69%	2.89%	2.39%	-1.91%	0.26%	7.40%	-2.14%	1.67%	0.00%	14.11%
2019	-0.26%	0.79%	-6.72%	0.31%	4.13%	1.31%	2.45%	-4.43%	-5.34%	-2.62%	-0.56%	3.89%	-7.46%
2020	-6.90%	-1.82%	0.00%	2.45%	4.96%	6.41%	12.04%	7.18%	-1.46%	-0.54%	11.13%	2.65%	40.42%
2021	6.69%	8.18%	-1.62%	1.92%	-3.60%	-5.72%	2.55%	-0.17%	-9.19%	5.16%	-5.20%	-1.71%	-4.19%
2022	-3.66%	0.00%	0.63%	-2.28%	0.00%.	0.00%	-2.57%	1.93%	0.00%	0.46%	5.88%	-2.41%	-2.35%
2023	4.75%	3.89%	-1.35%	1.81%	2.74%	2.50%	4.77%	-3.78%	-1.44%	0.08%	0.89%	-0.56%	14.83%
2024	4.81%	13.07%	6.58%	1.08%	-2.64%	-0.50%	0.907.	-2.92%	1.26%	0.00%	0.00%	0.00%	22.68%

Results of Combining Systems #5 and #6

	MR Long 1	MR Long Short Lookback	Combined 50% each
CAGR	16.6%	17.1%	**17.1%**
Maximum drawdown	21.1%	26.6%	**16.7%**
MAR	0.78	0.67	**1.02**

Because we are trading two systems in the same stock universe and the same style but with different filters, setups, rankings and exits, we get superior combined results. CAGR stays high, the maximum drawdown drops, and MAR improves. System #6 addresses the weakness we saw in System #5.

Is there anything else we can do to further diversify our mean reversion strategy?

Yes, there is. We can focus on a particular sector.

CHAPTER 10

SYSTEM #7: HEALTHCARE SECTOR MEAN REVERSION

WITH THIS SYSTEM, WE CAN TRADE A MORE VOLATILE SET OF stocks, and volatility will give us good options for mean reversion. Our first two mean reversion systems trade in the universe of all stocks, and our LTTF systems trade in the S&P 500, the NASDAQ, commodity ETFs, and energy stocks. Since we're seeking diversification, we'll focus on healthcare stocks.

Why healthcare? At certain times the healthcare sector is negatively correlated to the broader market, which is a good thing. (Think about what happened during the pandemic, when some healthcare stocks did exceptionally well.)

Objective

Buy stocks that have the possibility to be volatile and noncorrelating to the overall market, giving us many opportunities to profit through mean reversion.

Rules

• Trading universe: All healthcare stocks

- Filters
  - Minimum price: one US dollar.
  - Daily volume: 500,000 daily average over the last fifty days.
  - Minimum average daily range percent is above 4.

- Setups
  - Close of the stock is above the 150-day exponential moving average.
  - Seven-day ADX is above 25.
  - Today and yesterday the stock closed down.
  - Pullback measurement: the two-day Williams % R is below -70.
  - Rank stocks by lowest two-day return.

- Entry
  - Place a limit order the next day of 0.5 ATR (over the last ten days) below the previous close.

- Exit
  - Stop loss of 1 ATR (over the previous ten days).
  - The close of the two-day Williams % R is above -40.
  - If either of those happens, we exit next day, market on close.

Instead of using the average true range for volatility, we use the average daily range just to create a slightly differentiated filter. The lookback is 150 days. Remember that System #5 has a 252-day lookback, and System #6 has a 40-day lookback, so this is notably different. The 7-day ADX above 25 gives us volatility. The stock has closed down during the last two trading sessions, and we know it's oversold because the Williams % R is lower than -70. (Williams % R is a scale from 0 [completely overbought] to -100 [completely oversold].) With a two-day lookback and a threshold of -70, we know the stock is significantly oversold in the short term, making it a good candidate to revert to its mean. Finally, we rank the stocks by lowest two-day return.

As with our other mean reversion systems, we get in with a limit order of 0.5 ATR over the last ten days below the previous close (because we like beaten-down stocks, but in this system not too much).

We get out when the Williams % R improves to better than -40 or with a stop loss of 1 ATR (ten days). The improvement in the Williams score means the stock is reverting toward its mean. The stop loss protects us from excessive losses.

Results

- CAGR: 32.4 percent
- Maximum drawdown: 50.4 percent
- Longest drawdown: 43 months
- MAR: 0.64
- Winning trades: 59 percent

I bet that maximum drawdown caught your attention, didn't it? That may not look very appealing, but even a system like this can be useful in a portfolio of automated, noncorrelated systems. It's also a reminder that high compound annual growth return has its price. If you see results like this on your backtests, believe them. Results like this are actually good! If you build a system that has a high CAGR and a low drawdown, that's a red flag that you have over-optimized your system, and it won't perform nearly as well in reality. Reality is what we want to model, not wishful thinking. Reality requires us to pay the piper for compound growth performance with larger drawdowns.

This system trades a portfolio of very volatile stocks. Healthcare is an industry subject to sharp ups and downs. A company might announce the approval of a patent after hours and see its stock open 30 percent higher or more the next day. On the other hand, disappointing results from a clinical drug trial can tank a company's stock at the opening bell. These unexpected moves can result in a high CAGR, but the associated drawdowns are also high.

Equity Curve of System #7 Healthcare Sector Mean Reversion

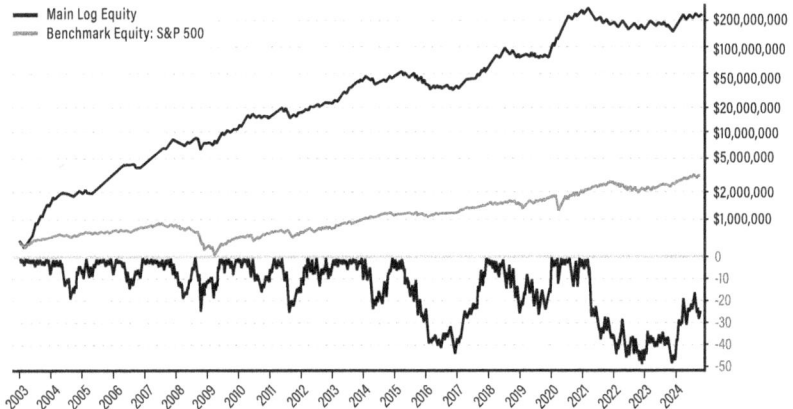

Notice that the system has been in drawdown since 2021, and as of the time I'm writing this book, it's still in drawdown. I include it as a reminder to keep your eye on your larger goal when you are building your systems. I see too many people build a system that underperforms in recent years and reject it, but that's a typical recency bias.

Most people suffer from this recency bias. When something hasn't worked for the last few years, they throw it away and go look for the next best thing. This is exactly what you are *not* supposed to do. Instead, accept time periods where a system does not work so well. Accept variability of returns.

It's dangerous because when someone sees this kind of a result on a backtest, they often are inclined to reoptimize the system, which can result in over-optimizing it. They end up with what looks like a better performing system, but it's not a representation of reality.

What matters is not a system's recent performance but when it makes money, when it loses money, and how that complements (or doesn't) your other systems. In real life you won't make money all the time with your systems, so it's perfectly normal, even advisable, to adopt systems that have performed poorly in recent markets so long as they make up for it somewhere else.

This system had big jumps in 2003 and 2020, and it paid the price for those with significant subsequent drawdowns.

Do you have the stomach for a system like this? Not everyone does, and you need to take a hard look in the mirror about your pain tolerance.

Here's how the backtests play out for the past twenty years.

Monthly and Annual Returns for System #7

As we've discussed, this is a volatile sector, and you get volatile results, some of them spectacular, like a 220 percent return in 2003 and 157 percent in 2023. On the other hand, there are times when it severely underperforms the benchmark SPY, such as in 2015, 2016, 2021, and 2023.

How does that make you feel? If you flinch, then this might not be the kind of system you want to trade. Can you handle a system that will buy individual stocks that are volatile in nature, can be low priced, and that might lose 80 percent? Can you handle being in drawdown for years or massively underperforming the broader market for extended periods?

If you see this as the product of a well-built system that is not over-optimized, maybe you'll like it. If you build a system like this, be vigilant about not over-optimizing it. If you are able to generate extraordinary results on a backtest by lowering the drawdown, that's a warning that you've probably built something that doesn't reflect reality. If you trade it live, you may be sorely disappointed in the results, which could lead you to suspend the system. That's an outcome we always want to avoid, and we avoid it by building systems that are as grounded in reality as we can make them.

The whole point of trading a system like this is that it generates dissimilar results from our other systems. So what happens when we combine all three of the mean reversion systems?

Year	Jan	Feb	Mar	Apr	May	Jun	Jul	Aug	Sep	Oct	Nov	Dec	Annual Gain	Benchmark
2003	1.21%	0.06%	5.60%	6.94%	19.45%	22.98%	14.46%	9.94%	13.23%	11.74%	16.17%	3.24%	220.76%	22.32%
2004	13.61%	6.04%	4.12%	0.74%	-1.23%	-4.86%	-3.21%	-2.23%	2.10%	6.49%	4.98%	-0.50%	27.64%	8.99%
2005	0.53%	3.21%	-4.94%	1.42%	0.64%	15.46%	1.82%	15.49%	9.49%	7.52%	2.66%	0.50%	66.01%	3.00%
2006	7.80%	5.99%	9.71%	-0.16%	-4.70%	-5.17%	0.66%	3.70%	0.73%	-1.35%	12.93%	6.50%	41.10%	13.62%
2007	3.29%	7.35%	5.45%	16.63%	4.13%	-3.62%	2.59%	5.77%	3.67%	12.42%	-0.98%	-1.98%	67.97%	3.53%
2008	-4.41%	-1.15%	-5.68%	0.04%	5.69%	3.56%	3.93%	4.16%	-5.61%	-10.52%	5.15%	5.18%	-1.32%	-38.49%
2009	0.48%	-6.10%	3.74%	4.53%	13.95%	8.61%	2.54%	4.85%	0.10%	-5.86%	5.66%	7.84%	46.17%	23.45%
2010	1.37%	10.27%	16.09%	5.81%	-0.67%	-0.22%	-2.15%	-0.86%	-3.38%	-0.27%	4.81%	-2.66%	29.77%	12.78%
2011	8.46%	9.09%	3.86%	0.49%	3.64%	-4.71%	-5.07%	-14.75%	3.12%	6.49%	2.07%	-1.88%	8.53%	0.00%
2012	11.60%	3.58%	10.74%	-1.02%	-1.09%	5.53%	-4.16%	3.88%	0.40%	1.70%	3.09%	2.89%	42.62%	13.41%
2013	-0.24%	2.00%	10.41%	4.43%	10.49%	5.04%	7.24%	12.39%	0.63%	1.76%	9.01%	-0.90%	81.55%	29.60%
2014	12.61%	-5.78%	-5.73%	-8.16%	-2.73%	7.55%	-6.47%	7.83%	-2.11%	13.11%	3.55%	5.11%	16.81%	11.39%
2015	2.20%	-2.36%	4.89%	-2.35%	-1.67%	-6.34%	3.21%	-4.84%	-8.78%	3.38%	-5.70%	2.42%	-15.79%	-0.73%
2016	-18.90%	-0.01%	0.10%	2.70%	-2.28%	-3.48%	7.72%	-1.62%	4.19%	-9.44%	-3.96%	1.89%	-23.08%	9.54%
2017	0.70%	13.53%	10.09%	0.95%	0.87%	0.09%	1.94%	12.11%	8.42%	-2.59%	15.53%	8.11%	93.36%	19.42%
2018	9.40%	11.78%	4.13%	-3.93%	7.85%	9.44%	-6.08%	5.40%	1.40%	-9.45%	1.91%	-10.85%	19.24%	-6.24%
2019	1.11%	5.04%	9.23%	-8.03%	2.67%	-0.85%	-7.64%	0.25%	0.22%	-0.25%	4.65%	27.23%	33.85%	28.88%
2020	10.01%	12.81%	13.25%	17.98%	17.87%	15.90%	5.23%	-1.73%	5.75%	-6.43%	13.02%	-1.65%	157.59%	16.26%
2021	14.21%	-1.18%	-8.28%	-9.23%	-5.15%	-8.77%	-4.63%	3.87%	1.14%	2.91%	-8.13%	-3.13%	-25.41%	26.89%
2022	-8.72%	5.34%	9.30%	-10.48%	-4.12%	-0.88%	10.97%	-10.44%	0.57%	0.10%	-10.88%	6.69%	-14.96%	-19.44%
2023	12.57%	1.75%	1.26%	-4.00%	1.83%	1.52%	-1.09%	-0.66%	3.28%	-16.48%	-1.32%	11.15%	7.00%	24.23%
2024	16.41%	2.64%	16.91%	-13.21%	7.52%	4.76%	4.89%	-7.43%	-3.29%	0.00%	0.00%	0.00%	28.24%	19.97%

Combined Results of Systems #5, #6, and #7 at 33.33%

	MR Long #1	MR Long #2	MR Long #3	Combined	S&P 500	Difference
CAGR	16.6%	17.1%	32.4%	**22.8%**	8.8%	14% more CAGR
Maximum drawdown	21.1%	25.6%	50.5%	**19.3%**	56.7%	37.4% less drawdown
MAR	0.78	0.67	0.64	**1.18**	0.16	1.02 better MAR

Equity Curve for Combined Systems #5, #6, and #7 at 33.33%

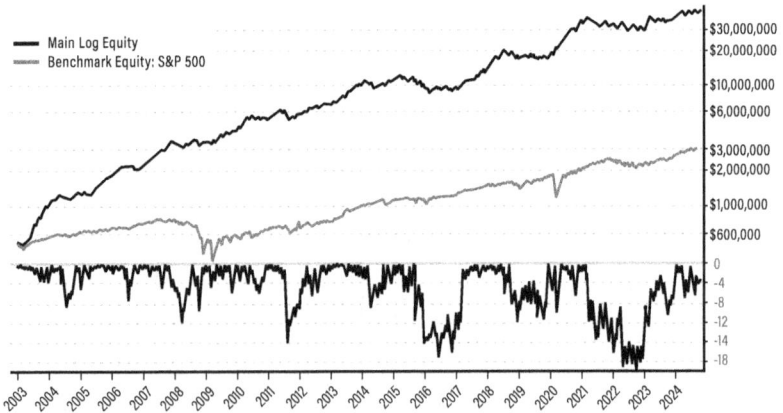

Individual Equity Curves for Systems #5, #6, and #7

Look at that: CAGR is almost 23 percent, the maximum drawdown is below 20 percent, and MAR is 1.18. Pay close attention to the last chart, and you can see why. The lower part of the chart shows the drawdowns and recovery records, which vary significantly between different systems. This is

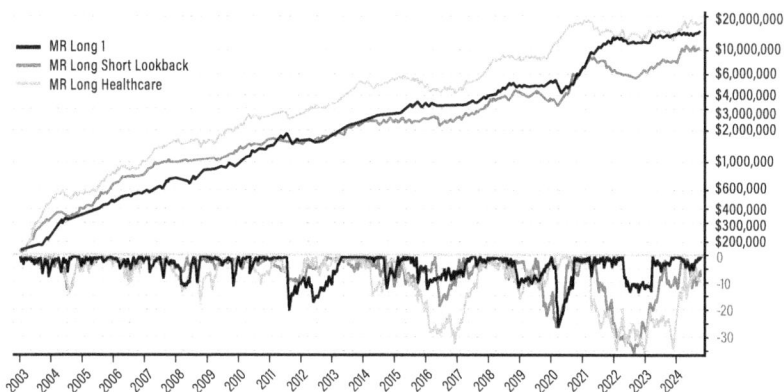

what we want to see. In the upper part of the chart, we see how they perform differently. For example, in 2023 the MR Short Lookback and "Catch a Falling Knife" systems did well, while the healthcare system was in drawdown. Perfect.

Looking at the previous chart (Equity Curve for Combined Systems #5, #6, and #7), pay attention to 2020: the COVID crash has been erased.

Three MR Systems Correlation Matrix

	MR Long #1	MR Long #2 Short Lookback	MR Long #3 Healthcare
MR Long #1	100	10.9	31.7
MR Long #2 Short Lookback	10.9	100	18.3
MR Long #3 Healthcare	31.7	18.3	100

CHAPTER 11

PUTTING IT ALL TOGETHER

WE'VE BUILT FOUR LONG-TERM TREND FOLLOWING SYSTEMS and three mean reversion systems. Because of the limitations on how retirement accounts can be traded, they all trade long, but we've done a good job in diversifying how they perform. So what does it look like when we put them all together?

We commit half of our assets to long-term trend following, putting 12.5 percent in each system. The three mean reversion systems each get 16.67 percent of our assets. Here's the result when we backtest from 2003:

Combined Results of Seven Systems

	Trend following 4 systems × 12.5%	Mean reversion 3 systems × 16.67%	Combined
CAGR	18.01%	22.80%	**20.41%**
Maximum drawdown	23.69%	19.34%	**15.81%**
MAR	0.76	1.18	**1.29**
Longest drawdown	29.6 months	34 months	**15.2 months**
Historic volatility	17.85	11.10	**12.39**

As expected, the combined systems produce the best results of all. But how do they compare against the benchmark?

	S&P 500	Combined	Difference
CAGR	8.86%	**20.41%**	11.55% more per year
Maximum drawdown	56.7%	**15.81%**	40.89% less
MAR	0.16	**1.29**	+1.13 more
Longest drawdown	65.4 months	**15.2 months**	50.2 months less
Historic volatility (100)	16.9	**12.39**	3.8 less volatile

Pretty well, don't you think? CAGR is more than double the benchmark, maximum drawdown is 40.89 percent less, the longest drawdown is a bit more than a year compared to more than five years, and our system is 3.8 points less volatile than the SPY.

Combined Equity Curve of Seven Systems

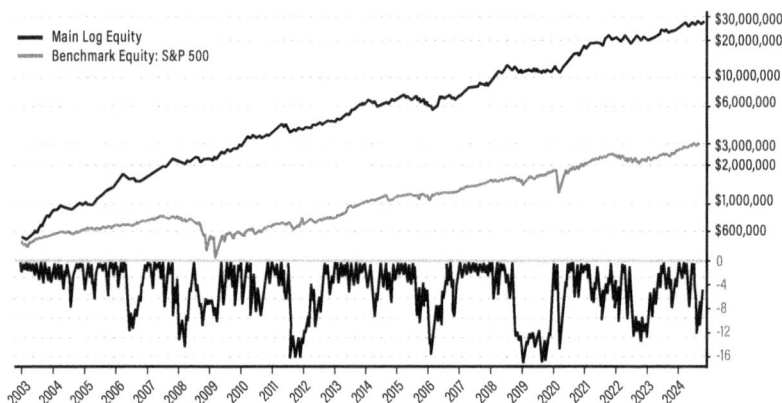

The equity curve tells the story of why our suite of systems outperforms the benchmark so well. The 2008 crash largely vanishes from our return profile. We still see declines in 2011, 2015, 2018, 2020, and 2022, but they are shallow and short. The 2020 decline in particular is notable because it is so much less severe than what the market as a whole experienced.

Twelve-Month Rolling Returns

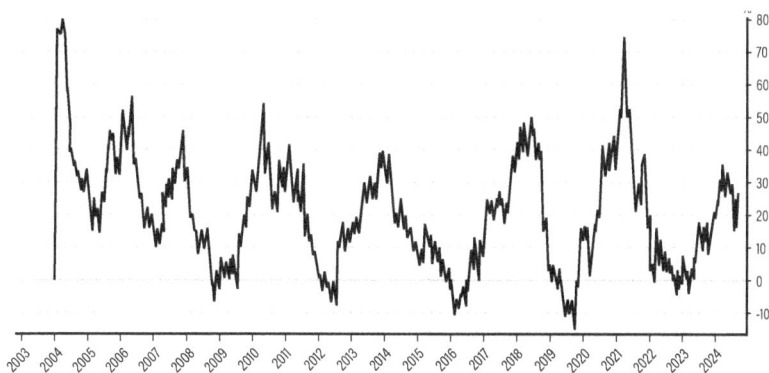

If we look at the twelve-month rolling returns, we see a steady cadence of rising and falling returns that rarely falls into the red, and that's important for our goals. I think this measurement is often overlooked as people tend to look at yearly returns, but this chart basically looks at every point twelve months back and logs the net return.

Historic Volatility Versus SPY

One of the key benefits of combining different styles, different portfolios, and different philosophies into a blend of

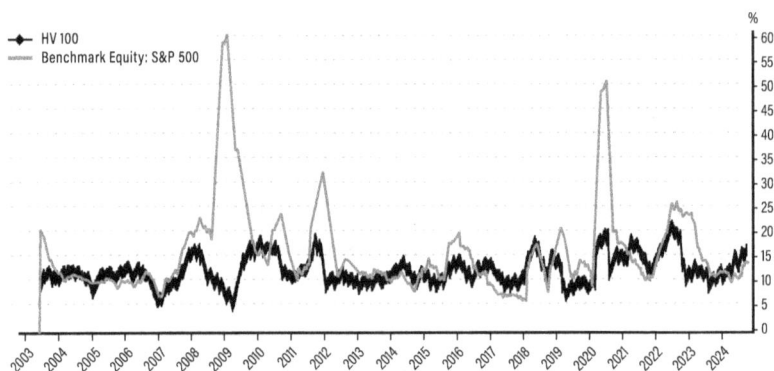

systems is that you not only smooth the equity curve, you also increase the risk-adjusted return and significantly lower the volatility of the equity curve.

If you take a look at the chart, you see that the historic volatility of the suite of systems is lower than the S&P 500—especially during market panics and crashes, when the volatility of the S&P 500 goes through the roof. This blend of system stays constant and in some cases even lowers the volatility. In 2008, when the panic was at its highest point, the volatility of the S&P 500 was ten times higher than our suite of systems. Imagine that you are trading your retirement money and all your peers are panicking in a buy-and-hold situation, but for you it is just another day where the P&L is not freaking you out.

If you're like most investors, you find volatility inside your portfolio to be stomach churning. This chart should give you comfort; when the S&P 500 was highly volatile, our suite of systems was not. In fact, it's substantially less volatile at all times.

Finally, let's look at the acid test: the annual returns.

Year	Jan	Feb	Mar	Apr	May	Jun	Jul	Aug	Sep	Oct	Nov	Dec	Annual Gain
2003	1.29%	-0.03%	2.05%	5.08%	9.45%	6.38%	4.31%	5.45%	2.12%	8.86%	3.39%	3.88%	66.03%
2004	5.03%	3.57%	1.09%	-0.74%	3.61%	1.20%	-2.71%	-2.51%	4.57%	4.98%	6.76%	0.89%	28.36%
2005	-1.50%	5.72%	-0.63%	-2.56%	2.33%	6.46%	5.23%	5.95%	4.90%	-1.18%	3.15%	3.14%	35.06%
2006	10.35%	-1.93%	4.03%	2.81%	-3.41%	-2.10%	-0.41%	1.22%	0.23%	1.62%	4.91%	0.39%	18.37%
2007	1.50%	2.32%	2.84%	7.00%	4.37%	-0.89%	-1.10%	2.90%	6.06%	6.69%	-4.38%	2.58%	33.50%
2008	-7.26%	1.11%	-2.75%	2.58%	5.90%	3.72%	-2.69%	-0.18%	-2.37%	-0.75%	0.91%	1.02%	-1.42%
2009	-0.45%	-2.07%	-1.10%	4.02%	6.94%	-1.39%	5.01%	2.28%	4.25%	-2.85%	5.08%	6.22%	28.40%
2010	-2.53%	6.26%	7.50%	5.41%	-2.81%	-3.22%	1.40%	-2.08%	4.73%	3.74%	5.37%	3.94%	30.44%
2011	4.39%	4.27%	2.72%	3.20%	-0.91%	-1.08%	0.41%	-10.59%	-1.87%	2.32%	-0.07%	-0.74%	1.12%
2012	2.59%	2.45%	4.99%	-0.67%	-3.64%	1.97%	-0.30%	4.22%	1.91%	-0.64%	0.94%	0.41%	14.83%
2013	4.14%	1.44%	4.91%	2.04%	4.54%	-0.42%	3.52%	1.48%	3.41%	2.97%	3.68%	1.70%	38.88%
2014	1.14%	3.25%	-3.17%	-0.36%	-0.15%	4.99%	-2.99%	4.95%	-1.60%	1.20%	2.27%	-0.13%	9.39%
2015	0.02%	1.87%	0.92%	-1.57%	3.12%	-1.64%	2.23%	-4.23%	-3.00%	3.87%	0.30%	-1.07%	0.47%
2016	-6.70%	-1.83%	3.01%	4.04%	-0.67%	1.03%	3.52%	1.47%	5.41%	-3.89%	1.43%	1.93%	8.39%
2017	1.75%	2.23%	3.80%	-0.05%	3.83%	0.32%	2.87%	2.31%	3.97%	3.36%	3.44%	4.64%	37.60%
2018	7.34%	1.41%	1.16%	0.51%	5.57%	2.38%	-2.15%	4.06%	2.20%	-9.62%	-0.32%	-3.69%	8.01%
2019	0.42%	1.40%	0.92%	0.17%	-1.57%	1.81%	-0.87%	-1.18%	-0.93%	1.28%	2.52%	10.03%	14.38%
2020	-0.68%	-1.14%	-4.30%	4.38%	4.20%	4.66%	8.25%	6.98%	-1.25%	-3.23%	9.79%	3.55%	34.56%
2021	6.56%	6.86%	-1.07%	1.38%	1.13%	-1.81%	-0.94%	1.69%	-1.18%	7.24%	-2.81%	1.12%	18.98%
2022	-2.62%	4.19%	6.07%	-4.42%	3.90%	-7.69%	1.80%	-0.78%	-2.34%	3.65%	0.06%	-1.82%	-0.91%
2023	4.03%	0.67%	2.65%	-0.52%	2.86%	4.17%	2.75%	-0.86%	-0.61%	-4.92%	3.66%	3.29%	17.62%
2024	7.81%	6.10%	6.60%	-4.69%	5.19%	2.17%	-1.00%	-3.85%	2.86%	0.00%	0.00%	0.00%	22.30%

Monthly and Annual Performance for Combined Seven Systems

The annual and monthly returns are telling. In twenty-two years of backtesting, this suite of systems made money for twenty years and barely lost money for two years. Remember our goals when we set out on this journey:

- Protect our capital.
- Beat the market.
- Hedge against inflation.

These charts show that, even with one hand tied behind your back as an investor who can't short stocks, you can achieve all three of these goals. Over twenty years, this suite of trading systems generated approximately 20X return, compared to approximately 6X return for the buy-and-hold strategy of the S&P 500 index. Even if you only achieved half of that in live trading, your life would be far richer, and far more secure, than if you had invested in the index.

Remember too that we made conservative estimates about the total return on your portfolio. We assumed you would be paid zero interest on your cash. In reality, you will earn interest on your cash if you trade with a brokerage that pays that. (You should; I have traded for years with Interactive Brokers, which as of the time of this writing paid 4.08 percent on cash balances.)

This is not an insignificant return. The chart below shows why.

Total Daily Exposure

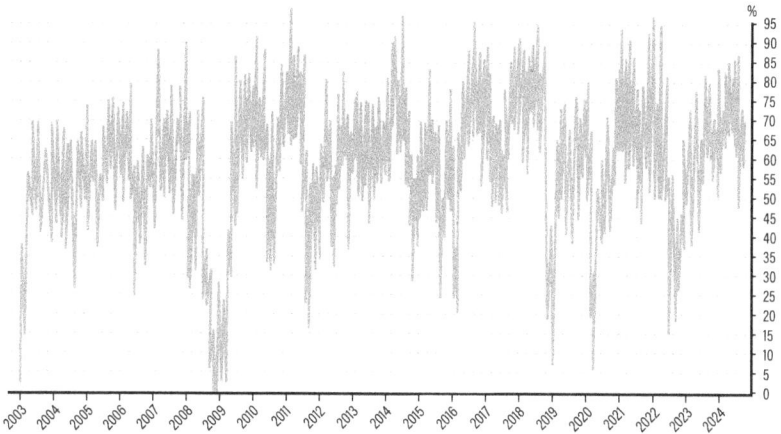

This chart shows how fully invested you have been in the market at any given time. You can see how when the market panics (look at late 2008, late 2018, March 2020, and 2022), your systems move to cash. The cash balance can (and should) be earning interest, which would have been about 4 percent. All of this adds to your total return on your portfolio, although we have not accounted for this cash balance in our simulations. It's frosting on the cake.

CHAPTER 12

BUILDING AUTOMATED TRADING SYSTEMS

EVERY HUMAN BEING HAS A DIFFERENT MIND. YES, WE SHARE many things in common, but each of us is unique, and that uniqueness extends to how we see the world, how we behave as traders, what makes us comfortable or uncomfortable. If you copy someone else's system, you likely won't stick with it because you have not worked on it, have not understood the philosophy underpinning it, have not seen its strengths and weaknesses. When it starts to move against you, you will abandon it. I've seen this happen time and time again.

Your suite of systems should reflect what you understand and what you are comfortable with. Some traders only trade long-term trend following systems. Some prefer mean reversion alone. I like to hedge against inflation with a portfolio of commodity ETFs. Some people like highly volatile stocks, others find themselves anxious about volatility. Or perhaps you want to trade only systems with higher percentages of winning trades, even if they are small, because that makes you feel better.

In other words, you are unique, and your approach to trading should be too.

When you build your own system, you know when it is supposed to make money and when it isn't, and you're psychologically much more likely to stay the course and keep trading it. Too many traders get into a drawdown of 10 percent or 15 percent for a few months and then suspend their systems. The more you understand when your system is likely not to do that well, the better you can stick with it and deal with the drawdowns. When you are prepared, you can stay in the game and not, like so many traders, suspend it at the worst possible time. I encourage my students to stick with a system for at least two years before they make a judgment about it. We all suffer from a powerful recency bias; it can be hard to have a long-term outlook when your new LTTF system has been losing money for six months. Plus, recency bias makes us forget that bad times happened and will happen again. I've heard people say things like, "I could have just bought the S&P 500, and I would have done great." That's true if you bought at the beginning of 2023. But they forget that it was down 20 percent in 2022, never mind 56 percent in 2008. Recency bias blinds us to history.

People suspend their system when the pain in dollars is more than they can handle. If I trade $10,000 and my system drops 20 percent, I'm down $2,000. That doesn't hurt too much. If I'm trading $10 million and it behaves exactly the same way, I'm down $2 million. It's harder for most people to remain calm about that, even though there is nothing wrong with the system and its behavior could be completely normal. Sticking with systems requires both discipline and faith, and that faith comes from building them yourself. It is incredibly important to think longer term, both backward and forward.

The best systematic traders in the world can be down for a year or two in a system and not worry about it at all.

Build Systems That You Trust

I often see readers and students try to replicate the systems in my book. This is not time well spent. If you have different software or a different data provider or different data format, if the software slightly interpretates the rules differently, or if you program it slightly differently, your results will be different, and you will spend endless months figuring that out. But what are you figuring out? You are trying to replicate the exact rules of a suite of systems that is now in public domain. As I said before, there is nothing special about the rules, nor is there about the indicators. *It is the concept that matters.* There can be hundreds of different variations of this.

I ask you to build your own systems because what works for me won't work for you. I recommend that you use what I teach in this book as a set of suggestions rather than prescriptions. You have your own biases and beliefs, and your systems should reflect those. With a clear understanding of your own objectives, of what you want to achieve in regard to trading returns and risk profile, and of the trading style that appeals to you, you can build a system that suits who you are. [1]

The result will be a trading system you will execute consistently with confidence and without fear or hesitation. You trust each system because you built it when you were in a

---

[1]   You can find detailed instructions about how to build your own systems, including understanding your own trading psychology, in my book *Automated Stock Trading Systems.*

calm emotional state. If your strategy accurately reflects your honest assessment of your risk tolerance and you are confident that the algorithm has an edge, then you don't need to worry. Your systems will make money and preserve your capital with little regard for market behavior. Once you build your suite of systems, your computer does the hard work. Critically, you are freed from making daily trading decisions. Enter rules into your trading systems and let the computer make trading decisions based on the facts of the market and the rules you have set up. You can create systems that trade every day, every week, every month, or every quarter—it's up to you and what you want to achieve.

The main thing I want you to do is understand the concepts that are the heart of this book. Combine multiple systems with the following:

- Different styles: mean reversion and trend following.

- Different portfolios and sectors.

- Different asset classes.

- Different rules per system, so you create different return streams.

- Use these tools to smooth the equity curve and lower your risk and volatility while increasing your possible return.

For Every System

For every system you build, ask yourself the following questions:

- **How does it fit into my overall strategy?** Each system should add strength to your equity curve.

- **What stock portfolio do I want to trade, and why?** This relates to your first answer.

- **What kind of price and volume filters do I want to use?** You might choose to trade lower-priced stocks because you believe there is an edge when you work outside the universe inhabited by big institutional traders.

- **When am I most comfortable entering a trade?** You may want to see the whole market rising, or you may be looking for a stock to be beaten down.

- **How do I want to enter a trade?** For example, a market order makes sense for an LTTF trade but not for a mean reversion trade where you may experience meaningful slippage.

- **When and how will I get out of a trade?** Always know why and how you will exit a trade.

- **What provision do I have to limit losses, and why?** A one-day automatic exit all but guarantees you won't be invested in a bear market. A 20 percent trailing stop gives a rising stock room to run. Each is part of a different objective.

- **When and how do I take profits?** Define a successful trade.

- **When do I exit?** On open or close, and why.

The Four Principles of Building Trading Systems

Make No Predictions
What the market will do is a mystery, so don't plan on it being otherwise. Create combinations of systems that will make money or at least protect your assets no matter how the market behaves.

Trade Only Backtested Systems
Only by working with solid data can you know if you have found an edge that will make money. Use a robust dataset to test your systems in all kinds of markets; don't cherry pick your dataset by excluding challenging time periods. Look for them to make money when they are supposed to and to lose money when they are supposed to.

Know Who You Are
Be mindful of your objectives and your risk tolerance. Because you must trade consistently, ensure that you trade in ways that make sense to you and are within your comfort zone.

The Future Will Not Be the Past

No system performs in live trading the way it does in a back-test, and no system consistently matches its predicted CAGR. Be conservative in your expectations, and take your projected returns with a healthy grain of salt.

But Wait—What About Bear Markets and Black Swans?

I started this book with the promise that I would show you how to do three things: make money in bull markets (and outperform the indices), protect your money in bear markets, and hedge against inflation. I've shown you how a suite of seven different systems can do that. But I've also been honest with you that sometimes uncorrelated systems will behave similarly, like in March 2020, when everything went down.

You might call that COVID crash a black swan event—an unpredictable, out-of-nowhere occurrence that shocks markets. Black swans are real, and they do happen. So do bear markets, and while our systems can limit your losses and protect your wealth in retirement accounts, they generally can't help you make (much) money in those accounts because of the regulatory limitations on short trading. You are much more likely to actually make money during bear markets if you can build systems specifically designed to take advantage of those market conditions and effectively trade short. Knowing this, some investors come to me with workaround ideas like trading inverse ETFs or volatility funds that are supposed to mimic short trading or trading short in another non-retirement account to offset the bear market exposure they may feel they have in their retirement accounts.

I have strong opinions about these ideas, and I've spent a lot of time studying them. However, an in-depth discussion of them is beyond the scope of this book, which is intended only to show the basic concepts of how to trade retirement accounts most effectively. If you are interested in learning more about these approaches, please turn to the back of the book for a link to a free video course I have developed that goes into these topics in depth.

CHAPTER 13

OVER TO YOU

I MEET SO MANY PEOPLE WHO ARE STRESSED OUT ABOUT THEIR trading, particularly when it comes to trading retirement accounts. One client told me about how he panicked during COVID and sold at the bottom of the market. Then, in the turndown in 2022, he panicked again and sold everything while in a 22 percent drawdown. He felt that if he focused every day and essentially worked as a day trader, he did all right, but he still had a regular job, and he couldn't do that consistently.

This is a typical variant on a common story. I hope this book has shown you that you don't have to live this way. You can build multiple automated, noncorrelated trading systems that will give you greater peace of mind, less volatility, and superior returns and protect your capital. As I have explained in my previous books, these systems can be automated to the point where all you do is execute the trades, or as I and some of my students have done, use software that connects to your broker while the complete operation runs on autopilot. Once the suite of systems is set up, that usually means spending thirty minutes a day entering orders. I trade fifty-five systems on autopilot, and my workload is minimized almost to zero.

My students and I enjoy many benefits from trading multiple automated noncorrelated systems. They include the following:

- Freedom! If you build a suite of systems like I have described and set it up to largely run itself, you are no longer chained to your computer. All you have to do is enter orders each day before the market opens, which typically takes between five and thirty minutes. You don't have to make judgments or second-guess yourself. Just follow the trading system's computerized directions and then go about your day. I cannot tell you how important it is to reclaim your time in this way.

- Ignore the financial press. It's an absolute relief to know that I don't have to pay attention to or care about what the media is saying today about this or that development in the markets because I literally don't have to care.

- Ignore the fundamentals. This is related to ignoring the media, since what they report on is almost always fundamentals—this or that earnings report—or a corporate event like a change in leadership. Since we don't use fundamentals in our strategy, that's just noise.

- Have a suite of strategies that are designed to make money consistently. You can earn consistent double-digit returns with the scale of those returns correlated to your risk tolerance.

- Experience smaller, shorter drawdowns. Your drawdowns can be notably less than those of the broader equity markets. Depending on your risk level, you can attain returns much better than a buy-and-hold strategy without even beginning to come close to the large drawdowns that strategy exposes you to.

- Stop worrying. This may be the most tangible benefit. It takes a while to attain it, because you have to watch your systems in the market and see how they actually perform, but as you learn to trust them, you can relax. I don't think it's possible to put a price on the peace of mind that comes from knowing you have done all that you can to secure your retirement against bear markets and inflation while also growing your wealth.

You won't attain all these benefits overnight. You can't do this halfway. You have to stick with it, and you *will* have down periods. Most traders fail because they lose their nerve and get out when the pain is too great. But if you are consistent, work hard at first, and have discipline, these benefits are very achievable. I've seen it happen again and again among my students. You will reclaim your time and your peace of mind—isn't that something worth working for?

If this sounds appealing, I encourage you to explore further. As I have mentioned, I wrote two books that go into the principles and procedures of trading automatic trading on noncorrelated systems, *Automated Stock Trading Systems: A Systematic Approach for Traders to Make Money in Bull, Bear and Sideways Markets* and *The 30-Minute Stock Trader: The Stress-Free Trading System for Financial Freedom*. I also highly recommend two other books: *Wealth Well Managed* by my business partner Alexei Rudometkin and *The All Weather Trader* by Tom Basso, with whom I teach an annual seminar. All are available from Amazon.

There are three ways forward from here, depending on your skills and resources:

Option 1: Build everything yourself. If you have excellent programming skills and want to build your own systems, this is a solid path. It takes time and dedication to build your own software, but you'll gain a deep understanding of your strategies and how they operate. For the right person, it can be a rewarding journey.

Option 2: Hire a programmer. If you're not a programmer (like me), hiring one might seem like the logical step. But unless you can clearly define exactly what you need, this route can be long, expensive, and frustrating. I personally spent over 18 years and well over $500,000 to create my own software. It's doable—but far from easy.

Option 3: Work with me. If you like my approach but feel overwhelmed by the idea of programming, testing, and executing your own system—and you want your own software that you can customize to your style, trade as many systems as you like, with no need to write a line of code, run everything on full automation, and get support building your strategies—then I can be your guide.

Take a look and see if it's the right fit for you:
tradingmasteryschool.com/elite-mentoring

A FREE GIFT FOR YOU

If you would like to learn more about how to prepare for and defend against black swan events, I have made a free video course in which I share my thoughts about what works, and what doesn't, when trading retirement accounts. In it I explain the following:

- The systems introduced in this book in greater depth.
- Why using inverse ETFs in your retirement account won't work the way the way you might expect.
- How to hedge your retirement account with a "sudden panic escape hatch" against moves like the COVID crash or the crash in August 2011.

- How to make money during catastrophic events like the 1929, 1987, and 2008 crashes (this involves trading on margin and trading short, two things you cannot do in a retirement account, or in some cases your broker might accept the usage of futures, but that goes beyond the scope of this book).

- Using mean reversion short and trend following short systems that will make money in bear markets (also limited to non-retirement accounts).

Access the video using this link:
tradingmasteryschool.com/book-offer

ACKNOWLEDGMENTS

THANKS FIRST AND FOREMOST TO MY BUSINESS PARTNER, Alexei Rudometkin, whom I first met when he came to me as a student. Trained as a nuclear scientist, he has a ferocious work ethic and quickly showed me his skills when he rebuilt the trading software that I had developed to make it easier and twenty times faster than ever to use. He has created the best software available for nonprogrammers to develop systems based on their personality, and he assists me in teaching my students, improving all our trading lives.

Market wizard and author Tom Basso is the person who inspired me to become a systematic trader in the first place. We have become good friends and teach a seminar together each year. I am grateful for his wisdom and advice, all of which have given me better balance in my trading life.

A sincere and heartfelt thanks to Hal Clifford, cofounder of Avocet Books. This is the third book we have worked on together. Hal has enormous expertise in creating books, tremendous skill with language, and endless patience with me. Writing a book by myself as a non-native English speaker would be impossible. Writing a book with Hal is an experience I look forward to in every call because I know he understands me, and I know we are creating something excellent.

Finally, my students keep me sharp, and that's why I keep teaching. I enjoy their incisive questions and the intense training sessions we have together. Being a trader can be a lonely occupation, and being a systematic trader even lonelier, because our approach is unusual and not easily understood. I am grateful for the community and camaraderie my students provide to me and to each other.

ABOUT THE AUTHOR

LAURENS BENSDORP IS THE FOUNDER AND CEO OF TRADING Mastery School and the author of two previous books: *The 30-Minute Stock Trader: The Stress-Free Trading Strategy for Financial Freedom* and *Automated Stock Trading Systems: A Systematic Approach to Make Money in Bull, Bear and Sideways Markets.*

He began his career as a whitewater rafting guide and instructor, working in Germany, Austria, Turkey, Israel, the Dominican Republic, Costa Rica, and Chile. In 2000 he sold his Mexican rafting company to work as an investment manager at a boutique firm in the Netherlands. Laurens undertook his own multi-year study of successful trading, educating himself about trading and risk management. He spent the next decade refining automated, algorithm-driven trading platforms to maximize profits while limiting risk and keeping management time to virtually zero. Since 2007, he has been trading systematically (now fifty-five systems, 100 percent on autopilot) and sharing his knowledge. His clients have included more than one hundred high net worth individuals, fund managers, and busy professionals who want to systematize their trading.

Fluent in six languages, Laurens travels frequently and has lived in more than a dozen countries. When he is not on the road, he divides his time between homes on the Mediterranean and in South America.

You can find me on *tradingmasteryschool.com* and follow me for market info and updates on: *x.com/laurensbensdorp*

www.ingramcontent.com/pod-product-compliance
Lightning Source LLC
Chambersburg PA
CBHW031858200326
41597CB00012B/469